THE BRAIN BENDERS

The Brain Benders

A STUDY OF THE EFFECTS OF ISOLATION

Second, Enlarged Edition

Charles A. Brownfield

Originally Published Under the Title
Isolation: Clinical and Experimental Approaches

An Exposition-University Book
EXPOSITION PRESS   NEW YORK

To the memory of T.H. Scott,

his widow, Margaret, and

their children.

BF
292
B7
1972

Originally published by Random House, Inc., as part of the Studies in Psychology Series
Second Edition

Manufactured in the United States of America
Library of Congress Catalog Card Number: 65-17441

SBN 0-682-47640-4 (cloth)

SBN 0-682-47643-9 (paper)

Published simultaneously in Canada

Foreword «‹‹

It is a tribute to the extraversion of modern Western man that he has taken so long to examine sensory isolation and deprivation. These conditions were not systematically studied until the last decade, except by an occasional prisoner or explorer who had been thrust into a situation where he was forced to face them. Yet this study is on the threshold of some critical questions. What adaptation is made to variations in, or an absence of, sensory input? What is left of mind itself when closed up within its own workings?

In contrast with extraverted modern Western man, who is bent on mastering the world about him, ancient man long ago ventured inward. Ancient meditators, ascetics, and others on religious quests deliberately withdrew from all sensory experience and even transcended awareness of their own body in order to open up the "inner rooms of the house of mind." The Hindu *Upanishads,* transcribed from a long oral tradition into written form before the Old Testament was written, has much to say on this subject. Early Buddhist, Christian, and other religious practices often followed this difficult route. I say "difficult" because there are a series of inner battles and discoveries to be made before the most interior aspects of the mind may be opened. The inward quest often takes years— years in which one hardly participates in the joys of the outer world. This path of "know thyself" is the difficult way to wisdom.

As scientists, we undertake the quest inward with conceptions, questions, purposes, methods, and instrumentation so different from those of ancient and Eastern man that our quest is of a different sort even though it explores the same territory. The ancients could not quickly transcend bodily awareness by long immersion in water because they did not have the necessary breathing apparatus, although it is likely that they would have done so had they had the equipment. There may have grown up conflicting schools; one advocating quick transcendence in water, and the other recommending the slower way—sitting in a cave. Likely too, the experience of transcendence would have meant something different to them than it does to us, because they conceived of scientific and religious issues as being grouped together in a single, little-differentiated frame of reference.

My colleague's summary in this book of the modern findings on isolation reminds me, again, of a lesson to be learned in science. It is our simple tendency to think that a definitive piece of research will settle a question. Yet, when the data are permitted to reveal their whole story (which doesn't happen if data are forced to fit preconceptions), they usually show that the territory explored is more complex than we presupposed it to be. So a search for truth reveals several or even many unexpected and unsettled possibilities. In this way science wanders through an increasingly complex territory, ever faced with more unknowns than at the beginning. This adds zest to the quest, for who would want to explore a forest that has boundaries and inner forms that were readily determinable? It would be like exploring a clump of

trees, not a forest. It can be said that the main difference between a scientist and a layman is that the
scientist's ignorance is far more differentiated than
the layman's; he knows better the boundaries of what
is not known.

The findings of sensory deprivation lie on the
threshold of the issues of the mind's inner workings,
its native tendencies, its native language, and the
question of the extent to which it determines itself.
It is something of an ancient axiom that if a man, in
overweening pride, thinks he governs his own mind,
the way to wisdom is for him to try to suspend its
operation. When he does, the more natural, inner,
spontaneous operations of the mind become manifest,
undermining the conception of his governing it. This
is not easy, for this, too, is a forest rather than a clump
of trees.

Wilson Van Dusen
University of California, Davis

Preface to the Second Edition ⋘

When this book was first published in 1965 as *Isolation: Clinical and Experimental Approaches,* it was meant to be an introduction to research and interest in sensory deprivation, perceptual isolation, and 'brainwashing" for undergraduate students, researchers just becoming interested in the field, and laymen who simply wanted to know what isolation was about without having to wade through a mass of technical details in various journals or in the multitude of published symposia then available. Apparently, I succeeded in my objectives, because the first edition sold out rapidly and reviewers felt the book did, indeed, have "something for everybody." At the urging of colleagues and students, and because I feel it still has something for everybody, I have prepared this second edition so the book is available again.

For advanced scholars who might wish to immerse themselves more deeply in detailed analyses of isolation phenomena, there is the excellent collection edited by Zubek (1969), and a major contribution by Schultz (1965), both of which I recommend highly to those who may want to know more after reading this work.

Since its initial publication, there has developed an interest in the relevance of research and theorizing about notions of general activation, arousal, optimal stimulation, and sensoristasis in dealing with isolation. Discussion of these concepts was intentionally omitted from the first edition, but because of increasing interest in psychophysiological ramifications of sensory and perceptual deprivation phenomena, I have decided to include here addenda dealing with these issues. These addenda are, perhaps, more technical than I had wished the general level of this book to be, but in line with my original intention of including something for everybody, and in view of the growing relevance of these concepts in understanding isolation, I have come to feel this material ought now to be included. My only suggestion is that the average reader may be more rewarded by reading the original text first and the addenda afterward.

1972   Charles A. Brownfield

Preface to the First Edition «««

Authors who write about scientific matters would like to feel that their efforts may provide a few answers to some questions; but the paradoxical nature of scientific discovery seems inevitably to raise a dozen new questions for every crudely approximated answer to an old one. It is thus anticipated (and earnestly hoped) that this attempt at presenting and integrating data will serve the heuristic purpose of generating many more questions than it answers and stimulating far more research than it reviews. For students, researchers, and merely interested readers, the issues associated with isolation, restricted early experience, brainwashing (as a procedure requiring a form of isolation for its effectiveness), sensory deprivation, and perceptual invariancy, have never failed to excite and capture the imagination; this is attested to by the ever-growing list of publications in these areas which have been accumulated during the relatively brief span of a decade since the first report of the original McGill University studies was published.

When I first began this book, I was motivated by the obvious need for an introductory text with a broadly based general reference source, to acquaint people just becoming interested in the field of isolation with what has been done so far and to stimulate new ideas for future investigation. I have tried briefly to cover the entire field as it has developed, without delving too deeply into the intricate and complex details of the differential research results. Hopefully this will spare the reader from having to wade through the mass of data which might justifiably have been presented. Instead I have concentrated on breadth rather than depth. The provision of a comprehensive reference bibliography is designed to allow the student to approach the literature of isolation in more than just the chancy fashion that has always characterized the initial phase of familiarizing one's self with a specialized research area. It is particularly true of isolation research which, like an awkward and ungainly adolescent, has grown too fast and in too many directions at once to have had the time to get organized and co-ordinated. This book is an attempt to help bring such an organization about; it is not the first such attempt nor will it be the last, but it is part of the effort at making a start on the introductory level.

The decision to include the material on brainwashing was prompted by many considerations. Foremost among these was the historical accident in which brainwashing and experimental isolation somehow got intertwined and associated with each other. There is some question now about the relevance of brainwashing techniques to the experimental reduction or elimination of external sensory stimulation. However, there is an overlap between the two, observable in the social isolation components of both situations, and thus the treatment of isolation phenomena may legitimately subsume brainwashing and justify its inclusion here, if only to dispel some of the misconceptions.

It has often occurred to me that my own interest in isolation phenomena, and consequently the motivation to write this little book, might never have come about had it not been for one brief but profound meeting with the late Dr. T. H. Scott on a warm Chicago evening in 1955. Perhaps the contribution which Harry Scott might have made had he lived will in some small measure be compensated for by my own interest and efforts in the area which he helped to start by his early participation in the original McGill studies. In this event I should like to think of this work as a kind of memorial to him and an extension of his contribution, even though I may have struck out in different directions than he might have done because of the differences between us in background, intellect, interest, and training. I have thus divorced myself from the credit for any merits which might accrue to this work—they belong to Harry Scott; I take full responsibility, however, for any faults or defects—these are truly my own. My appreciation is also extended to the American Psychological Association for permission to reprint, in revised and enlarged form, materials in Chapters 5, 6, and 7 which first appeared in *Psychological Bulletin*, 1964, *61,* 304-313, and to Professor Koji Sato of Kyoto University, Japan, for permission to incorporate in Chapters 6, 7, and 8 revised material first published in *Psychologia,* 1964, 7, 63-93.

Finally, I would be remiss if I did not acknowledge my gratitude to Dr. Wilson Van Dusen, without whose encouragement and insistence I might not have undertaken this work; to Dr. Rudolf Holzinger, for his lively, enthusiastic, and critical discussions of the manuscript and for his moral support so graciously given; to Dr. L. Joseph Stone, for his valuable advice in the organization of the book; and to my wife, Constantia, for the dual role she played in preparing the manuscript and running interference between me and our two vivacious children.

Ukiah, California   *C.A.B.*
September, 1964

Contents ⫷

Part 1 ⋘⋘⋘

The Psychopathology
of the Solitary Mind

The great object of life is sensation—
to feel that we exist, even though in pain.
It is that "craving void" which drives us
to gaming, to travel, to intemperate but
keenly felt pursuits of any description,
whose principal attraction is the agitation
inseparable from their accomplishment.

—George Gordon, *Lord Byron*

CHAPTER 1

Introduction

The past decade has witnessed a rapid development and expansion of scientific interest in the consequences of isolating a human being from all the familiar elements of his sensory world. Deprived of vision, hearing, touch, heat-and-cold sensitivity, smell, taste, and the pervasive feel of the pull of gravity on the muscles, we ask how a conscious person would react to that "craving void of nothingness": that profound disengagement from normal sensory and perceptual experience? Might it become a threat to his very awareness of existence? Such awareness, after all, *might* depend upon the ability to feel and to respond to stimulation mediated by the organs of external sensation, *i.e.,* the eyes, ears, nose, mouth, skin, etc. Would these conditions, tantamount to psychological "suspended animation," preserve the intellect, or would the lack of stimulation to the brain, through the complex network of the nervous system, result in some change in mental function? Can isolation from the usual relationship with environment change people's attitudes or their basic outlooks on life, turn them into mindless ciphers, drive them insane, or cure them of mental illness? Oddly, all of these and other results have been alleged to occur when the mind, or more correctly, the brain, has been put into solitary sensory confinement. It is one of the purposes of this book to discover just how much of this is fact.

Isolation and Brainwashing Origins

Beginning in the early 1950's, toward the close of the Korean War, the question of what happened to people when they were isolated in a social vacuum , captured the imagination of scientists and the general' public alike. Some saw here a key that might open the door to some of the many mysteries of human existence and functioning; others saw only the vague, sinister threat of a diabolically clever but subtle psychological weapon for menticide (Meerloo, 1954). The experiences of American prisoners of war in North Korea reinforced this latter notion.

In view of the Chinese Communist "indoctrination program" and its seeming success in warping the attitudes of Americans so that they collaborated, defected to communism, or remained inordinately subservient in captivity (Farber, Harlow, and West, 1957; Lifton, 1954, 1956a, 1956b; Segal, 1954, 1956; Strassman, Thaler and Schein, 1956), gross and fanciful misconceptions were engendered which ultimately led to the belief that a new and irresistible technique had been developed which caused some prisoners to think and act in conformity with Communist expectations and others to be driven to mental incompetency (Kinkead, 1957; Meerloo, 1954, 1956).

The idea that something strange, sinister, and incomprehensible must have taken place in those internment camps north of the 38th Parallel persisted for some time. The sense of helplessness and fear created by our ignorance of the methods by which the Chinese accomplished their *thought reform* (Lifton, 1956a, 1956b) and subversion of Americans rested uneasily in the minds of those who heard the disconcerting news reports. With the return of prisoners of war under "Operation Big Switch," however, and with the opportunity to question and evaluate the repatriates' experiences, a variety of reports slowly appeared in the popular and psychiatric literature, some of which confused, but most of which clarified the real·nature of what actually had taken place (Biderman, 1956; Santucci and Winokur, 1955; Segal, 1954; Strassman, Thaler and Schein, 1956; and others). Yet even while this snail's-pace process of clarification was going on, a peculiar combination of events occurred, with the result that a somewhat misleading and even more mysterious-sounding label was to be applied to the then-nameless techniques utilized by the Communists. This label was *brainwashing* (*cf.* Hunter, 1953) —and the sequence and combination of these events is quite interesting.

The Mindszenty Affair

On December 26, 1948, Cardinal Jozsef Mindszenty of Hungary was arrested in Esztergom and charged with plotting against the Communist government, spying, treason, and black-market dealings in currency. When he was brought to trial on February 3, 1949, this high prelate confessed to the acts he was charged with and was subsequently sentenced to life imprisonment (later commuted). Prior to his arrest, and apparently anticipating his trial and conviction, the Cardinal had written that any confession he might make would be forced and not genuine. During his public trial, however, he seemingly confessed of his own volition, making no protestations of his innocence and co-operating fully with his accusers. The non-communist Western world, astounded, sought credible explanations, recalling similar phenomena witnessed in the Soviet purge trials of the 1930's. Observers at the Cardinal's trial pointed out that he had appeared haggard, and that his behavior was strange, as if he had been subjected to some kind of torture, drugs, or possibly hypnosis. While these suggestions were plausible, they remained largely unsubstantiated; and the effect was to give the impression that the Communist accusers had developed some secret method with which they could effectively control the thought, actions, and behavior of even their staunchest adversaries. Such a prospect was indeed quite unnerving.

The Korean Period

With the advent of the Korean conflict, the employment of psychologically effective stratagems by the Communists in combat became extensive. Newspapers published accounts of American prisoners collaborating with the Chinese by confessing to atrocities such as germ warfare, the killing of innocent civilians, and a variety of other acts which, to Americans, sounded absurd. Captured Americans were reported to be defecting to the enemy or developing sympathies for communism, and the same disconcerting specter evidenced in the Cardinal Mindszenty affair reappeared.

However, as we have noted, conclusions were reached before all the facts were known, and were based largely upon the experience of one individual who was singled out by his Communist captors for rather special and abusive treatment because he was a general (Dean, 1954). By and large, his experiences were not typical of those of 99 percent of the other prisoners; but his story, together with a few isolated and also atypical accounts from other captives, lent impetus to the imaginative speculations that a secret weapon was being utilized to break men's minds and cause them to become Communists or Communist sympathizers (Hinkle and Wolff, 1956, 1957).

Behavioral Organization

Concurrent with these dramatic, world-shaking events were some relatively obscure and (by comparison) rather commonplace developments destined to have a profound bearing on conceptions of the coercive activities in Hungary, Korea, China, and elsewhere. In 1949, Donald O. Hebb published his book, *The Organization of Human Behavior,* in which he attempted to explain the function of the central nervous system in the light of recent psychological and physiological experimental findings. Hebb proposed a nontraditional, theoretical, and neurophysiological model of the central nervous system. His thesis involved a revision of perceptual theory which, although at variance with a major assumption of Gestalt psychology, was congruent with both psychological fact and the seeming central direction of behavior. Acknowledging the fact that some determinants of perception were innate or unlearned, as the Gestaltists maintained, Hebb qualified this by attempting to show that even "simple" perceptions are actually more complex than had been surmised—that "they are additive" and "depend partly on motor activity, and their apparent simplicity is only the end result of a long learning process" (Hebb, 1949, p. 17).

Extensively referring to the works of von Senden (1932) and Riesen (1947), Hebb stressed the effects of early experience with deprivation of vision and other sense modalities on perceptual behavior. He credited the Gestaltists with providing the psychological evidence which challenged the oversimplified neurophysiological "switchboard theories" of Behaviorism

(Solomon, Kubzansky, Leiderman, Mendelson, Trumbull and Wexler, 1961, p. 2). Hebb's own theoretical formulation stressed the total field of brain activity with its neuronal networks, reverberating circuits, feedback mechanisms, and the probabilistic basis of its operation. As he elaborated on this, he specifically considered the effects of monotony on later-learned behavior. He hypothesized that monotonous, unchanging stimulation resulted in a disorganization of the ability and capacity to think. He attributed the disorganization to interference with "phase sequence" functioning in the brain (Hebb, 1949, p. 226). New content, in the form of continually varying sensory stimulation, was needed for the phase sequence to maintain its organization of combinations of cell assemblies at a normal level of excitability and persistence. Thus, stressing the type and patterning of sensory stimulation, Hebb reasoned that in the absence of varied stimulation, brain functioning would become impaired.

Sensory Deprivation

At about the same time that Hebb was writing his book, a graduate student at Ohio State University submitted a doctoral dissertation dealing with the effects of *sensory deprivation* on subsequent discriminative perception by men in different compartments of a learning apparatus (Bakan, 1949). It was the first time that the term sensory deprivation was used in professional literature to describe a procedure that denied an organism normal, complex sensory stimulation from the external environment for a specified period, yielding results that indicated such an experience made a difference in perception, as Hebb was suggesting. Under Hebb's direction the term was later applied more encompassingly to experimental isolation procedures with humans at McGill University in Canada (Bexton, Heron, and Scott, 1954; Doane, 1955, 1959; Heron, Bexton, and Hebb, 1953; Heron, Doane, and Scott, 1956; Heron, 1957; Scott, 1954; Scott, Bexton, Heron, and Doane, 1959). It was at this point in time that the term *brainwashing* entered our common vocabulary (Hunter, 1953), and it soon became connected with the McGill work, at first without much justification. By monotonizing the sensory environment, in the manner suggested by the McGill University studies, the experimental research with sensory deprivation suggested that human subjects would behave differently from their previously characteristic patterns. This *seemed* to be precisely what had happened to Cardinal Mindszenty and to the American prisoners of war in North Korea. Many popular writers, and even scientists who were not beyond being influenced by the popular press, began assuming that some form of intentional sensory deprivation might have been involved in brainwashing. For a time, some erroneously regarded the two terms synonymously. The McGill group, however, did not make this connection at first; they addressed themselves only to the experimental verification of Hebb's theory of phase sequence organization and to some parallel practical problems of the efficiency decrements noted in people exposed to certain repetitive tasks in military situations. Citing Mackworth's studies of human efficiency under conditions which demanded prolonged vigilance and attention (Mackworth, 1950), the McGill investigators proceeded to isolate their subjects in a sound-attenuated cubicle in which there was constant, invariant masking noise, low level of illumination, unpatterned vision produced by translucent goggles, reduced tactual stimulation, and restricted opportunity for movement. The results of their tests suggested that there was disorganization of thinking, as Hebb predicted; but it remained for other researchers to enlarge and qualify these findings which received rather widespread and sensational coverage in newspapers and magazines, once the link between these conditions and brainwashing was proposed.

Isolation and Man's Needs

In order to grasp the phenomenon of isolation and the background which catapulted the whole question of brainwashing and sensory deprivation into the realm of scientific inquiry—and the public imagination—we must approach the problem first from a relatively simple and naïve viewpoint. Human beings are always confronted with two major, irreducibly basic problems: (1) the development and preservation of ourselves as individuals; (2) the preservation of our kind in the continuation of the species. To be successful in coping with these tasks, we must depend upon our environment, including other people, in order to survive and later, to find an appropriate mate. Man, then, must be a social creature for his own emotional and mental health, because of the importance of the social environment in enabling him to meet his biological needs (Hebb, 1955).

Success in meeting most of life's basic needs involves becoming responsive to appropriate cues from the physical and social milieu in which we live. This can only be done through the sensory apparatus—sight, touch, hearing, muscle sense, temperature receptors, occasionally smell and taste—and all combined in the form of complex perceptions. Such complex perceptions remain with us through life at various levels of recall, aiding us with our primary task of survival.

Sometimes inappropriate perceptions taking the form of misinterpretations or distortions of reality lead to poor judgment; if persistent and inflexible enough, this may lead to a state of emotional imbalance. People have even committed suicide because they believed in or acted upon false, delusionary, misleading perceptual cues. These false cues can be mild and take the form of irrational fears, anxieties, phobias, and uncontrolled impulses; but when severe enough they involve gross distortions of reality as in psychosis (insanity). In studying man, we are interested in assessing how these various sources of sensory stimulation lead to appropriate social behavior and contribute to man's physical, mental, and emotional well-being. If this can be done, we may gain further insight into the nature of man, perhaps thereby enabling us to provide the optimal conditions for his growth, development, safety, and survival.

To be alone, cut off from familiar things and other people, is an experience that is both sought and feared, depending upon what expectancies, values, and goals one imputes to the situation. Some can be terribly disturbed by the stress-laden condition of loneliness; others, as we shall see, seek it out intentionally, finding in it comfort or the secret to a new integration of the personality. Differences between people—in this context—are of paramount importance in understanding the differences in the response to being isolated (Arnhoff, Leon and Brownfield, 1962; Parry, 1960; Brownfield, 1964a, 1964b).

Analysis of "Isolation"

In thinking more critically about *isolation* we may note that there are different kinds of isolation situations which are of major concern in both civilian and military affairs today, especially in connection with the current space research activities of the Air Force.

These fall into four general categories: (1) *confine-ment* to a limited space; (2) *separation* from particular persons, places, or things for which the individual has attachment and dependency needs; (3) *removal* from the total environment (*i.e.*, both social and sensory) by the reduction or elimination of stimulation; and (4) the *monotonizing* of stimulation—making it so invariable that it is no longer perceived (Helson, 1947, 1948; Sells, 1961).

The essential principle of *confinement* is restraint of freedom of movement. This can be accomplished by a seat belt, a shoulder harness, a strait jacket, barriers like a wall, a locked door, a threat or command, or encapsulation in a pressure suit and in the sealed cabin of a space vehicle. Similar psychological conditions can be produced by time restrictions such as a curfew or a deadline.

Separation from a particular set of persons, places, or things (as stimuli) to which the individual is attached, or upon which he is dependent, may be a result of distance or duties which keep one away from home, having communications disrupted, delayed, or eliminated, or receiving limited or censored information. Sometimes it may involve the loss by death of a loved one, upon whom the bereaved was emotionally dependent, thus accounting for some of the symptoms of grief.

Being cut off or *removed* from the environment is a situation that will exist in the sealed-cabin ecology of the spaceship, and which now exists in the operational tasks required in airplanes, submarines, weather stations, and radar watches. It is evident in solitary confinement conditions, as well as in some of the sensory deprivation research studies with which we shall presently deal. It frequently involves both confinement and social isolation, but only insofar as they are part and parcel of the reduction or relative absence of normal levels of sensory stimulation.

It has also been shown that when a stimulus becomes *monotonous,* unchanging, invariable, and boring, that stimulus loses its ability to evoke a response —it is adapted to, and not consciously perceived— almost as if it did not exist (Helson, 1947, 1948; Jasper, 1958). For instance, soldiers have learned to sleep during long artillery barrages, not being disturbed or awakened until the noise stops, causing a change in the level of stimulation. It is the change in the noise level, and not the noise, that causes a response. We shall have occasion to return to this point again.

Any or all of these conditions may be fulfilled by internal states, such as restraint by fear, conscience, principle, voluntary deprivation, and self-punishment. External factors—impoverished early experience, weakness or injury, physical reduction of sensory abilities such as vision and hearing, the social withdrawal of the aged, or the sudden, painful loss of a specific sense organ—may also produce isolation phenomena and consequent changes in mental functioning.

CHAPTER *2* «««

Anecdotal Reports of
Isolation Experiences

Consider now the reports of shipwrecked or solitary
sailors, explorers, and prisoners of war who either voluntarily or involuntarily spent long periods of time
alone. There are also anthropological and historical
anecdotes.

Admiral Richard Byrd, in his book *Alone* (Byrd,
1938), relates his experience of being isolated for six
months in a small hut buried under the snow in the
Antarctic. He originally undertook this voluntary confinement in order "to taste peace and quiet and solitude long enough to find out how good they really
are." But for Byrd, life in the polar night, snowed in,
in the confining, monotonous, unchanging surround-
ings of a small space, with little or no sound from
outside, and nothing to look at or see out there in any
event, changed from tranquil serenity to a lurid
nightmare existence. There were complicating factors
too: bone-chilling cold, the danger of carbon mon-
oxide poisoning from a defective heating stove, the
ever imminent possibility of the roof collapsing, the
fear that he would not be rescued in time, and finally
the overwhelming apathy which affected him so that
he was barely able to bring himself to tend to the

necessities of eating, drinking, and keeping warm. He lay in bed, unmotivated, hallucinating, and experiencing all sorts of bizarre ideas. After three months alone, he found himself becoming severely depressed. He "felt a tremendous need for stimuli from the outside world, and yearned for sounds, smells, voices and touch." He experienced, as have many others who have undergone similar isolation, an "oceanic" feeling —that almost pleasant state of being "at one" with the universe, of losing the sense of one's identity as an individual, of floating freely through timeless space like some disembodied spirit.

Christiane Ritter (*A Woman in the Polar Night*) was exposed to isolation for periods up to sixteen days at a time (Ritter, 1954). She reported bizarre experiences similar to Byrd's—hallucinating monsters, developing a monomania to go out over the snow and expose herself, seeing her past life in a vision, as if in bright sunlight, and feeling "at one" with the moon. She was rescued and tenderly protected from doing herself harm by an experienced Norwegian who put her to bed and fed her lavishly. She thus had another person with whom to share her feelings, something Byrd lacked. Strangely, she developed a kind of love for the situation, and was reluctant to leave Spitzbergen and the fascination of isolation with its attendant mental symptoms. This "love," which others have also experienced, seems similar in some ways to the pleasures derived by drug addicts and the "anaesthetic revelations" described by William James in *The Varieties of Religious Experience* (James, 1902). Interestingly enough, Norwegians and other peoples of the lonely northern reaches who have had similar experiences in Spitzbergen and elsewhere, more or less accept what we call *psychotic episodes* as normal experiences as long as the person does not destroy himself or someone else. They expect people to hallucinate under these conditions and they have learned empirical rules of thumb for treating them (Brainard, 1929; Clark and Graybiel, 1957; Scott, 1953).

Eskimo fishermen will not venture out in their kayaks alone, but will go only with other fishermen so that they can call to each other, laugh, joke, and generally stimulate one another in order to keep themselves in touch with reality. Those who have gone out alone have been known either to hallucinate, or, because of the stultifying sameness of the snowscape combined with the rhythmic movement of paddling the boat, to lapse into a hypnotic trancelike state and keep paddling until they sail far out to sea without hope of getting back. A similar phenomenon involving disorientation and loss of ego boundaries has been observed among skin-divers; this is called "rapture of the deep".

On the other hand, Truk Islanders of the Western Pacific make long trips in sailing canoes, rarely alone, it is true, on which they frequently get blown off course by a storm or typhoon. They lack any modern navigation system and operate on dead reckoning; once off their course they are lost. As a result of this, or as a result of being becalmed or carried away by the current, they spend long periods of time in the boats, alone or in small groups, with all the usual conditions of isolation and exposure. From reports of those who have reached shore, there has never been any suggestion of aggressive, self-destructive, or weird behavioral experiences of psychotic or other origin. Nor have hallucinatory episodes been related, though these are culturally acceptable. Under normal circumstances a Trukese is rather expected to see ghosts if he goes out alone at night. There is also a concept of insanity—even a word for it—and the criteria for calling someone insane are rather liberal. Yet even though such behavior is expected and accepted, no lost Trukese voyagers have admitted experiencing it (Lilly, 1956).

Solitary sailors are actually in a more complex and stimulating situation than the polar isolates. Sailing a small boat across large oceans requires a great deal of physical and mental exertion, and this, together with lack of sleep, poor nutrition, and exposure to the ravages of wind, water, heat and cold, and social isolation can also cause mental symptoms. Dr. Alain Bombard (Bombard, 1953), a French physician studying nutrition, spent sixty-five days on a life raft, subsisting solely on the food he caught from the sea. He relates that the first days are the most dangerous ones; he experienced awe, humility, and stark fear in the face of the mammoth expanse of ocean in which he was barely a microscopic speck. If the terror of the first week can be managed and overcome, states Bombard, one can survive. Like Byrd, he reported that he "wanted terribly to have someone who would confirm any impressions, or better still argue about them." He needed someone to confirm his very existence! He began to feel that he would be incapable of discerning between true and false, between reality and fantasy. Also like Byrd, he used the same techniques to fight off depression: efforts at controlling his thoughts, forcing himself to concentrate, dwelling on pleasant memories, and refusing to think about the dangerous, anxiety-provoking aspects of his situation.

Once the frightening first week is passed, other symptoms begin to develop, either from social isolation or from the combination of isolation and other stresses. Joshua Slocum (Slocum, 1900), a solitary sailor in the South Atlantic, had a severe *mal de mer* just before a strong gale hit his vessel. He had reefed his sails but knew that he should have taken them down,

sick or not. Under these circumstances, he was incapable of moving from his cabin during the storm. At
one point he saw a man take over the tiller, though he
knew this couldn't be, for he was alone! Then he
thought it was a pirate; but the stranger reassured
him, revealing himself to be the pilot of one of
Columbus' ships, the *Pinta,* who would take the boat
safely through the storm. Slocum pleaded with him
to take down sail, but the man refused, indicating
that they must catch up with the *Pinta* somewhere
ahead. The following morning Slocum recovered and
found that his little boat had covered ninety-three
miles on true course, sailing itself. The boat was per-
fectly capable of such a feat and Slocum could rig it
this way for long trips without his hand having to be
at the helm; however, in a dream that night Slocum
saw the pilot again, and was told that he would come
whenever needed. During the next three years the
phantom helmsman appeared several times during
blows.

This "savior" type of hallucination or delusion is
apparently quite characteristic of the strong egos that
survive the seemingly hopeless stresses of isolation,
loneliness, and exposure. This is in contrast to the
"destroyer" type of hallucination experienced by
those who do not survive, and reported by those who
do. The inner conviction that one will survive appears
typical of the healthy mind even under stress.

Walter Gibson (Gibson, 1953) was on a ship in the
Indian Ocean during World War II. This ship was
torpedoed and Gibson found himself one of a hun-
dred and thirty-five survivors crowded into a lifeboat
bobbing aimlessly in the midst of a vast expanse of
open water. He gives a vivid account of his experiences in his book, *The Boat,* relating the effects of loss
of hope, physical hardships, food deprivation, thirst,

scorching sun, and the consequent irascibility and violence which broke out among the unfortunates. Almost everyone hallucinated rescue planes and drank salt water, thinking it was fresh. Many became depressed and committed suicide; others were murdered, and some were eaten by people-turned-cannibal out of desperation, hunger, and the will to survive. Some personalities were destroyed and some were rebuilt and restructured in pathetic efforts at clinging to life. Many who committed suicide by jumping overboard first attempted to sink the boat by removing the drain plugs; these demented souls felt the need for the destruction of others as well as themselves. Such efforts at taking others to death along with them may have occurred in many cases of non-survivors who did live after a sinking but ultimately perished, never leaving a trace. This may also account for those transoceanic voyages in small boats by two or three sailors who never reached their destinations.

Gibson was ultimately one of only four survivors of that terrible ordeal in the lifeboat in which 131 other people aboard perished! Why did he live and the others die? He claims that his success was due partly to having become immunized to the ravages of the tropical sun by years of experience and training out-of-doors, partly by having learned to become completely passive (mentally and physically) in his responses to events going on around him, and partly by never doubting his deep and abiding conviction that he would come through this harrowing experience alive. He also had the intimate companionship of a woman survivor, Doris Lim, who shared his passivity and convictions; they bolstered each other's spirits and each reinforced the other's will to live. In almost all survivors of similar disasters, we find this inner conviction that one will survive, or the definite reassurance from others that each will be rescued. Apparently people can convince themselves of greater security, much as is done in some autosuggestion techniques.

On this point of conviction, it should be noted that a similar mechanism, related to hypnotic suggestion, operates to integrate as well as disintegrate the ego. Suggestion, or rather human beings' susceptibility to suggestion, can also have beneficial therapeutic effects, as shown in the current practices of treating the mentally ill. This is so because many systems of treatment rely on the individual's proneness to implication or suggestion. A psychologist (Allport, 1955) once remarked that scientists may have a very impressive formula or equation describing the orbit of a planet around the sun; such an equation may be inaccurate, but this does not make a bit of difference to that planet as it swings merrily on its way. This is not true of human beings, however, for once one imposes an "equation of human behavior," or an idea of how humans should behave regardless of its validity, people do everything they can to conform to it. Huxley, in *The Devils of Loudun* (Huxley, 1952), dramatically describes the effects of just such suggestion in seventeenth-century France and the hysterical belief that one is "possessed" of demons. He also notes the case of a priest-exorcist, Surin, who was convinced that he too had become infested by demons and was driven to the depths of psychotic depression and despair, withdrawing and isolating himself almost completely from the world. He remained in this tortured state for many years until another kindly priest-confessor said to him, simply yet profoundly, "You will recognize your mistake, you will be able to think and act like other men, you will die in peace." From that moment on "the suffocating cloud of fear and misery began to lift"; only then did Surin begin to recover.

Other kinds of symptoms reportedly manifest themselves in response to isolation situations; among these are superstitiousness, intense love of any living thing, conversations with inanimate objects, and the feeling that one might be considered insane when returned to civilization. As examples, Slocum thought a dangerous reef named "M" Reef was somehow lucky because *M* is the thirteenth letter of the alphabet and thirteen was his lucky number; he was also sickened by the idea of killing food-animals, especially a goat that had been presented to him at one port. Bombard imagined that the number of matches needed to light his damp cigarette symbolized the number of days remaining until the end of his voyage—he was wrong several times; he also had conversations with a doll he had brought along. Patrick Ellam and Colin Mudie (Ellam and Mudie, 1953), two voyagers sailing together, became grossly disturbed after catching and eating a fish that followed the boat all day, so they swore off fish-eating afterward. Louis Bernicot (Bernicot, 1953), after crossing the Atlantic alone, refused an invitation to dinner on another boat until he could recapture the appropriate mood of gregariousness and find the proper things to talk about. In isolation, the inner feelings become so vivid and intense that it takes some time to readjust to life among other people and to re-establish a conventional criterion of sanity (Lilly, 1956).

So far, most of these so-called *psychotic episodes* have been reported as occurring in survivors and seamen who were alone. Jean Merrien in *The Solitary Navigator* (Merrien, 1954), relates 185 different cases.

He makes the point in his introduction that, in going through the relevant literature, he found that it was better to be alone in some cases than to have another person along. It was also better to have three people than to have two; two people can get very much involved with each other, as was the case of de Bisschop and Tatibouet, where psychotic behavior did develop. They crossed the Pacific from China to Hawaii, and then to the United States. Tatibouet was secretly stealing the rations both had, eating part of them and throwing the remains into the sea so that de Bisschop would not know. Finally, there were no rations left. Fortunately, within a couple of days they were within sight of land, and were thus saved from starvation. De Bisschop forgave Tatibouet for his behavior because he was so overcome with emotion by the fact that it was his birthday and Tatibouet had saved half a biscuit to give him as a present.

Christopher Burney (Burney, 1952), a British army officer captured by the Germans in France, spent nearly eighteen months in solitary confinement. When placed once more among other prisoners, he was afraid to speak for fear of showing himself insane. Only after several days of listening did he recapture the normal sense of propriety and allow himself to speak. He related that while in confinement he "felt a sense of impotence, an inexorable subjection to a machine of nameless horror." Burney summarized his thoughts about isolation succinctly: "Variety is the very stuff of life. We need the constant ebb and flow of sensations, thought, perception, action and emotion —keeping even our stability in the ocean of reality." The story of Robert Stroud, "The Birdman of Alcatraz" (Gaddis, 1958), will attest to the tremendous drive that can be aroused in an individual for the stimulation of activity. Stroud, in solitary confinement for fifty-six years, became a literate, active, productive expert on birds, experimental research, penology, and criminology. He was urged toward intense study by the need to overcome the boredom and monotony that threatened to overcome him, and he was allowed all the material with which to accomplish this.

Charles Dickens, too, noted the debilitating, terror-laden effects that social isolation and restriction of the senses can cause. In his description of his visit to the Philadelphia Prison in 1842, he portrayed the profound mental aberrations that can result:

> This prison was conducted in a plan peculiar to the State of Pennsylvania. The system here is rigid, strict, and hopeless solitary confinement. Standing at the central point and looking down these dreary passages, the still repose and quiet that prevails is awful. Occasionally there is a drowsy sound from some lone weaver's shuttle, or some shoemaker's last, but it is stifled by thick walls, and heavy dungeon door, and only serves to make the stillness more profound. Over the head and face of every prisoner who comes into the melancholy house, a black hood is drawn, and in this dark shroud, an emblem of the curtain dropped between him and the living world, he is led to the cell from which he never again comes forth, until his whole term of imprisonment has expired. He is a man buried alive, to be dug out in the slow round of years, and in the meantime dead to everything but torturing anxieties and horrible despair.

He describes a number of the inmates in detail:

> The first man I saw was seated at his loom, at work. He had been there six years. He stopped his work when we went in, took off his spectacles, and answered freely to everything that was said to him, always with a strange kind of pause first, and in a low, thoughtful voice. "And time goes pretty quickly?" "Time is very long, gentlemen,

within these four walls." He gazed about him and in the act of doing so fell into a strange stare as if he had forgotten something.

In another cell was a German, sentenced to five years for larceny, two of which had just expired. He had painted every inch of the walls and ceiling quite beautifully. The taste and ingenuity he had displayed in everything were most extraordinary, and yet a more dejected, brokenhearted, wretched creature, it would be difficult to imagine. I never saw such a picture of forlorn affliction and distress of mind.

There was a sailor who had been there upwards of eleven years. "I am very glad to hear your time is nearly out." What does he say? Nothing! Why does he stare at his hands and pick the flesh open upon his fingers, and raise his eyes for an instant, every now and then to those bare walls which have seen his head turn grey?

(Dickens, 1898)

In 1900, Maurice Small summarized much of the then-known data about the relationship between social life and solitude and the mind's dependency on these. Small thus seems to be one of the earliest forerunners of the scientific study of isolation phenomena; He made the following observation:

All knowledge of self and things is relative. Personal orientation depends largely on objects in the visual field. In the presence of a desert, a prairie, a sea, or the sky; in an absolutely dark cavern, or on the summit of a mountain, a feeling of disproportionateness between the man and what he sees overwhelms consciousness. Paralysis of association results. Retrogression to a half-vegetative state, like that of infancy, follows. If the eyes be open, they do not see. They have neither fixation point nor accommodation. Their gaze is as vacant as in the early days after birth, as stolid as the frozen state that follows death. All the life there is, lies within. When that which has seemed real, abiding and certain in the objective field becomes blank, the psychic condition passes rapidly through a change whose nearest analogue is the bladder of air in a receiver from which air is being exhausted. In the effort to expand itself to the range of its new conditions, the self finds itself only a loosely related mass of reflexes from experience, distrusts their coherence and their affinities, sees the flitting nature of consciousness, loses itself in the Unknown.

(Small, 1900, p. 39)

More recent examination of the consequences of isolation, solitude, deprivation of the senses, and similar phenomena has failed to substantiate Small's pessimistic generalizations and predictions, although his conceptions fit nicely into the brainwashing paradigm and probably played a significant role in producing the initial fears and misconceptions about it.

Positive Features

Henry David Thoreau looked at the world of his time and came to the conclusion which he made the cardinal hypothesis for his famous dissertation on self-reliance and individualism: "The mass of men lead lives of quiet desperation." Rather than advocate closer and more intimate relationships between people, he sought freedom for the self by demonstrating how effective and happy a person could be by himself, without the dependency, frustration, and stress of trying always to please others by fulfilling the manifold prescriptions and proscriptions of society. He sought freedom within himself by withdrawing from the world of people—alleviating his loneliness by isolating himself from those human interactions which he felt made men quietly desperate and lonely. In so doing, he did what many others have done in order to discover some basic truths.

Moses, for one, withdrew from the multitude of the

Hebrews to spend forty days and nights alone on Mount Sinai, returning ultimately with the revealed truths of God's Law. Upon his return, in anger at discovering the people had turned to the worship of an idol, the Golden Calf, he smashed the tablets and had to return again to the solitude of the mountain top where he obtained another set of tablets. While the Bible frequently associates ideas of separation, exile, and being cut off from one's group with expressions of fear, yet in many other instances it associates isolation with spiritual renaissance and revelation, such as the receiving of the Ten Commandments. John the Baptist grew up in the isolation of the wilderness desert, developing the highly ascetic mysticism of the future Christian movement. Jesus himself went out into the wilds to be alone and free of the distracting influences of the world, there to suffer the inner temptations of Satan which He had to overcome so that He might begin His great ministry. The apostle Paul also spent some three years in the desert of Arabia, learning God's teachings by the inner promptings that could only be heard in solitude. Mohammed, too, underwent similar isolation. The trance-states of the Hindu, Zen, and other Eastern mystics are, in this sense, a withdrawal from the world and the body with the goal of experiencing complete "awareness" and "enlightenment," which is achieved only by the renunciation of involvement in and concern with material, worldly, and bodily matters, *i.e.*, the "self." The retreat into monasteries by adherents of various religious orders is a professed effort to shut out the world and to experience a transcendence to spiritual existence—to allay loneliness by achieving a sense of closeness to, and friendship with, God. Even among these orders it is common practice to spend some period of time alone in a hermitage, on a vigil to seek one's true vocation—to experience, if possible, a miraculous revelation of one's true calling and purpose in life. Some American Indian tribes, as well as other materially primitive groups, would sometimes send young men out alone into the desert so that they could hallucinate or otherwise actively experience a supernatural phenomenon. This was part of a maturity rite, after which the young men were accepted into the ranks of adults. High value, in each of these examples, is placed on having such experiences, and it was intuitively recognized that they were only to be had alone, in the quietude of isolation. In some inscrutable way the person who undergoes such a transcendence is considered better off because of it—he is honored, and therefore fulfilled in life.

The Biblical injunction to "Be still, and know that I am God" (Psalm 46:10) has been taken literally—particularly, but not exclusively, by Eastern religions—as a guide to achieving that enlightenment (or knowledge of God) which many seek. "Stillness," in this context, appears to mean the exhaustion and suppression of all physical and mental activity, the elimination of the ego and its boundaries, and the consequent dawning, it is claimed, of awareness (or "pure consciousness") of what is actually so obvious that, but for the interruptions of external sensory stimulation from the world and our personal, egocentric concerns, we should all be aware of it (God). That "still, small voice" which apparently cries out continually in the hustle and bustle wilderness of our daily physical and mental lives can be heard, some say, if we simply "be still." It is this insight that prompts spiritually motivated people to find the means by which to achieve the stillness thus prescribed.

It would seem that a kind of dissociative process is required to arrive at the desired state of stillness—a process which ultimately entails the disengagement of physical sense perception from interaction with the external world of stimulation. This is apparently done by certain of the physical exercises of Yoga, accompanied by a line of reasoning that may facilitate the dissociative process psychologically. Since nothing can exist, goes the reasoning, outside of God, all things, creatures, and people, are "one in God." Thus enlightenment also involves the realization of one's "oneness" with the Almighty—that, in fact, all things are manifestations of God, including the person who perceives this. Once this perception occurs there is no further need for anxiety, questioning, doubt, or wonder. Since man is a manifestation of God and thus, in an internal sense, *is* God ("I and my Father are one"), all problems cease to exist. Thus, when asked what heaven was like, Jesus answered in the best yogic tradition (say the yogis) that "the kingdom of heaven is within you." It is precisely the contemplation of this almost axiomatic statement which prompts some religiously motivated people to seek out and experience heaven within themselves by eliminating external sense perception and worldly social interactions so that they may discover the internal "bliss" (Merton, 1960, 1961). Yogis, perhaps more than any other group in the world, practice a form of self-imposed sensory deprivation that far exceeds that of a research laboratory. Unfortunately, this aspect of the problem has not received much serious attention from psychological, physiological, and neurological investigators, but we can allude to these practices in passing, and hope the future will yield more interest and organized investigation.

One of the more extraordinary cases of revelation and spiritual enhancement reportedly brought about by attaining a "state of bodily insensibility" (an apparent dissociative state requiring disengagement of sensory receptivity from the environment) was that of Emanuel Swedenborg (1688—1772), an accomplished and universal-minded scientist of the caliber of Newton, Galton, and Harvey. He wrote voluminously on a variety of scientific and mathematical subjects, achieved universal fame and recognition, and was active in the politics and finances of Sweden. At the age of fifty he retired as Assessor of the Swedish Royal Board of Mines to begin a career of religious revelation through massive but anonymous literary production (*see* Trobridge, 1945). Swedenborg professed to have been allowed by the Lord to have free communication with spirits and angels and to see and comprehend the secrets of Heaven and Hell. His claims seem to be supported by fairly well-documented evidence from historical contemporaries attesting to his unusual powers of clairvoyance, mediumship, philosophical and theological acumen; and his writings did (and do) have a peculiar appeal to intellectuals noted for their logical abilities, creativity, and sense of moral justice. Swedenborg himself observed that once free of bodily sensibility (physical sensation) his spirit was enabled to fathom the secrets of life and God; he advanced the interesting theory that all sensations were derivatives of touch, a notion that has gained increasing support through years of scientific investigation, especially with the development of microbiology and the knowledge of unspecialized one-celled organisms which respond to light, heat, cold, touch, and other stimuli without benefit of specialized receptors. The phenomenon of *synesthesia* (the ability to experience sensation not ordinarily evoked by a specific stimulus, *e.g.*, to "see" colors when music is played, or "hear" sounds when visual stimuli are present) lends credence to this idea. It has been suggested that Swedenborg unwittingly practiced certain yogic techniques involving bodily dissociation and thus experienced mental phenomena which he attributed to divine intervention and which some of his followers called "Enlightenment."

Dr. John C. Lilly, in examining various reports of isolation effects from such autobiographical material as was available, concluded the following:

(1) Published autobiographies are of necessity incomplete. Social taboos, discretion to one's self, suppression and repression of painful or uncomfortable material, secondary elaboration, and rationalization severely limit the scope of material available.

(2) Despite these limitations, we find that persons in isolation experience many, if not all, of the symptoms of the mentally ill.

(3) In those that survive, the symptoms can be reversible. How easily reversible, we do not know. Most survivors report, after several weeks' exposure to isolation, a new inner security and a new integration of themselves on a deep and basic level.

(4) The underlying mechanisms are obscure. It is obvious that inner factors in the mind tend to be projected outward, that some of the mind's activity which is usually reality-bound now becomes free to turn to fantasy and ultimately to hallucination and delusion. It is as if the laws of thought are projected into the realm of the laws of inanimate matter and of the universe. . . . Such experiences either lead to improved mental functioning or to destruction. Why one person takes the healthy path and another the sick one is yet not clear.

(Lilly, 1956)

Civilization and Loneliness

In isolation from the physical world of which we are a part, we allow primary processes—basic, undisguised mental functions, impulses, fantasies, etc.—to come to the surface (or they come whether we "allow" them or not). Sometimes the experience is devastating, but sometimes it does lead to feelings of greater security; and the new integration, as reported by those who have been so exposed, depends upon how one was initially prepared to accept it.

Civilization is an ongoing attempt to dispel man's basic sense of loneliness and insulation by utilizing that primary attribute of gregariousness that characterizes man as belonging, for survival purposes, among other socially organized life forms. We have constructed an elaborate, complex, and intricate system of social existence which makes life more convenient and comfortable than in the primitive state; and this system, together with the physical world within which it exists, provides us with a perceptual frame of reference to interpret the data of our senses. By banding together in groups, cultures, societies, or governments, we maximize the opportunity for fulfilling our biological needs through social communication; but we give up some of our uniqueness of thought and perception in the process of conforming to expected standards. We develop superficial secondary processes in order to conform, taking these to be reality rather than realizing that they are only part of it. Our vacillating abient, and adient impulses, the natural concomitants of artificially imposed controls on our behavior, express themselves in confused, conflicting, and often neurotic interpretations of reality. We all, then, tend to insulate ourselves from the realization that we do work at cross-purposes with our natural impulses; to this extent we cut ourselves off from the mainstream of human unity, in the defensive maneuver to preserve our frequently mistaken ideal of an integrated ego. Thus we are lonely and we feel a vague, gnawing sense of abandonment despite our efforts to the contrary. Civilization, then, has not only failed to dispel our anxiety of loneliness, it has served to magnify it. Hebb (1949) aptly points out that the more advanced and complex civilization has gotten to be, the more prone the civilized mind has become to greater irrationalities and anxieties—more so than the so-called primitive mind which, contrary to popular opinion, functions more on the level of primary processes, with greater suggestibility and magical thinking. While "uncivilized" people are superstitious and inclined to think of the world in magical terms, civilized minds are subject to these same foibles and tendencies *plus* all the conflicts and real, logical concerns of the anxiety-provoking civilized world.

CHAPTER *3* «««

Men Against the Mind: Brainwashing in China

In the preceding discussion of isolation, we have touched several times on that topic popularly referred to as *brainwashing* (coined by a newspaperman named Hunter in 1953). The phenomenon is not new, though the word itself is relatively new. Nor is it mysterious, sinister, or irresistible once the facts are brought to light. The undeserved dignity lent to it by ignorance and uncertainty makes brainwashing seem like magic and thus may, through the mechanisms of suggestion, allow it to have some validity. Methods of forceful indoctrination and persuasive coercion, the principles of which were known and practiced as early as the fifteenth century (Group for the Advancement of Psychiatry [GAP], Institores and Sprenger, 1928), can be analyzed and understood simply as deliberate attempts to change behavior and attitudes by a group of men who have virtually complete control of the environment in which their captives live. Their victims are, in a special sense, isolated from those sources of consensual validation which normally reinforce their value standards and, consequently, their behavior. The result is to create a kind of hypersuggestibility and receptivity to reinforcement of new values and expectancies because there is no way, other than that permitted by those in control, to confirm a judgment. Similar attempts to change people can encompass such widely diverse areas of activity as education, advertising, rehabilitation in a prison or reformatory, religious conversion, and psychiatric treatment in a mental hospital (Bone, 1957; Gaddis, 1958; Packard, 1957; Schein, 1962). If similar methods are being used by the Communists in their so-called "ideological reform" (Ai Ssu-chi, 1951), it may well be that they have drawn upon the same reservoir of human wisdom that we have, but applied this knowledge to purposes that our society cannot condone. Nor can we condemn our own methods simply because they resemble brainwashing; for there may be something of value to us in our efforts to understand human beings.

The purpose of this and the following chapter is to summarize some of the factual evidence about brainwashing as it has been accumulated and studied over the years since it first drew public attention. In this way, the reader may begin to comprehend the use to which isolation, particularly of the social type, has been put in order to affect behavior change (*cf.* Zimmer and Meltzer, 1957). To do this topic justice, however, is an impossible task within the limited scope of this book. Thus the reader is directed to the references in the Bibliography if he wishes to pursue this fascinating subject in greater depth. From the present work, it is hoped that one may begin to see the relationship between man's dependence upon stimulation from the external environment for the maintenance of normal thinking, and how alteration or distortion of that environment can alter or otherwise distort thinking and behavior. The relation between brainwashing and isolation should become more apparent as we proceed.

The First Intimations

George Orwell's *Nineteen Eighty-Four* (Orwell, 1949) was a classic novel and a disturbing handbook for brainwashers as well. The hero (or victim) of the story, Winston Smith, was subjected to the interminable abuses of social isolation, solitary confinement, starvation, sleeplessness and probably sensory deprivation, physical beatings, personal betrayal and humiliation, drugs, torture, and direct electrical stimulation to the brain. He was made to feel utterly helpless, with no chance of being rescued because there were no would-be rescuers. He felt that the Party could and would control his thinking, and that ultimately he would love nothing but the Party. The story, which received widespread publicity, is so convincing that many people who read the book, saw the movie or television versions, or even heard about it, tended to interpret any type of involuntary indoctrination, including radio and television commercials, as a variant form of the "scientific" process suggested in the story. It seemed that Orwell gave us a prototypic glimpse of what the future might be like if the world persisted in the direction which the book extended to its extreme yet almost logical conclusion. Even before the term "brainwashing" was coined, we read of the indoctrinator saying to his victim, Smith, "We make the brain perfect before we blow it up. No one whom we bring to this place ever stands out against us. Everyone is washed clean. There is nothing left in them except sorrow for what they have done and love of the Party. It is touching to see how they love the Party. They beg to be shot quickly so that they can die while their minds are still clean." But Winston Smith was not shot, thus providing us with a peculiar parallel to be enlarged upon here. It was apparently much more fruitful to change or convert opponents of the Party than to eliminate them completely.

The Lenient Policy

Both the Russian and the Chinese Communists learned from their experiences in the 1920's, 1930's, and 1940's that a lenient and moralistic approach to prisoners was much more likely to elicit co-operation than the authoritarian, threatening, physically abusive methods commonly thought to be effective (Ai Ssu-chi, 1951; Beck and Godin, 1951; GAP, 1957; Hinkle and Wolff, 1956; Hinkle, 1957; Hinkle and Wolff, 1957a; Hunter, 1953; Jordan, 1957; Krivitzky, 1939; Lermolo, 1955). Not mere leniency, but a well-calculated program of inconsistent, somewhat confusing, and alternately threatening treatment was found to be the best combination of behaviors; if generously interspersed with kindness, it had the same conditioning effect that an inconsistent parent has on a submissive and consequently overdependent child (Meerloo, 1954). This approach is generally supported and reinforced by Oriental culture, which demands submissiveness and obedience to elders and parents and contains much moralistic and humanistic philosophy. Confucianism, for example, has always emphasized the importance of self-cultivation and reform, and while Chinese Communist leaders condemn Confucius and the older philosophies as too "idealistic," they often cite both Confucius and Mencius as examples in self-motivated reform for good Communists to follow (GAP, 1957).

There are so many aspects to the complex and manifold influences in thought reform that it is difficult to label any particular practice as definitely arising from Confucianism, Buddhism, or Christianity, although even these influences are very definitely found in brainwashing. All advocate, in one form or another, social justice, confession, and reform for the good of the soul, a change in attitude by the spirit of social responsibility, and so forth. All propose to accomplish these admirable transformations by nonviolence, reason, and faith. This is not to imply that the doctrine of nonviolence is characteristic of world communism—only that, for purposes of changing peoples' attitudes in a favorable direction toward communism or for manipulating behavior, the Communists themselves have found lenient, nonviolent methods combined with some experience of violence and alternate threats to be more effective than killing or maiming people. They have also discovered that by treating their prisoners as "students," *i.e.*, according them a certain dignity and respect as well-meaning but misguided people in need of re-education, they were more apt to win converts to their cause. This is a disarmingly logical and efficient way to spread an idea. The zeal of the convert is a well-established phenomenon in religious matters; for communism to have zealous advocates of its cause, especially where there were none before, is quite an ideological achievement and asset.

Here, rather dramatically, is the parallel between *Nineteen Eighty-Four* and thought reform: it is more desirable to maintain the victims—prisoners or "students"—alive because they are considered potentially more valuable to the state or Party when they are won over. In actual fact, in order to achieve this position the Communists had to liquidate or eliminate a relatively small proportion of their population which was considered too radical, subversive, or resistant to change; these were generally the former leaders or, paradoxically, the criminals among them. Once these people were eliminated, however, it was fairly easy to establish thought reform programs.

Neither the Chinese nor the Russian Communists appear to have used any organized psychology, in the Western sense of the word, though some of our scientists and even some of theirs have attempted to rationalize their methods in terms of one system or another (usually Pavlovian). The cultural heritage of the East, however, is frequently overlooked. Eastern religion and philosophy have always emphasized human relationships; and the Chinese, particularly, have become especially skillful in learning how to meet the psychological needs of other people and to manipulate them. Thought reform or "brainwashing" in this sense may be a perversion of a cultural talent with the goal of achieving communist aims rather than aims that would have been the natural consequence of traditional Chinese culture. Thus, while current methods of reform may seem discontinuous with the culture, they are also outgrowths of that culture. The Chinese, like most civilized peoples, are generously endowed with liberality, gentleness, and leniency, despite the rather false stereotype usually maintained of them as being sinister, inscrutable, sadistic, and villainous. American, or Western, attitudes toward Oriental captivity were shaped largely by the experiences of prisoners of war under the Japanese during World War II and partially by rather vicious Oriental stereotypes of the Fu Manchu genre. The Chinese, if they seem to act in a villainous and warlike way, may actually be so now, subsequent to having been influenced by some Western ideas—not the least among which was communism, a political, social, and economic theory propounded first by a nineteenth-century German named Karl Marx.

The Subversion of Ideas

Since the Chinese Communists have established themselves as *the* government on the mainland of China, they have been conducting a program of consolidation, re-education, and indoctrination which has aroused considerable interest and anxiety in the West. A similar process has been going on inside the Soviet Union since the successful revolution of 1917. Theories of moral degeneration or Chinese (or Soviet) Communist omnipotence both fall short as explanations of why the phenomenon of political conversion or ideological reform has been so successfully instituted; but when examined in the appropriate context, the reasons will become more apparent.

Intensive and formal thought reform programs for Chinese intellectuals were initiated and conducted in special institutions known as "revolutionary colleges." These were established all over the country immediately after the Communist takeover in 1949. It should be emphasized, however, that thought reform methods were not concentrated only on intellectuals in the special centers to be described; they were also applied, in varying degrees of intensity, to those in more formal university settings, in labor organizations, in business and government groups, and even to the peasants—in fact, throughout the enormous population of China. The seeming success of this process was a rather astounding achievement and well worth studying for the lessons we can learn from it. It will also serve as an introduction and clarification of the so-called brainwashing that later took place during the Korean Conflict, and which relied heavily upon social isolation for its effectiveness in controlling prisoners.

The Revolutionary Colleges

The revolutionary college drew its student body from among former Nationalist officials and teachers under the old regime, Communist Party members who had displayed "errors" in their thinking or activities or who had spent lengthy periods of time in Nationalist territory, from students returning from studies in Western countries, and from arbitrarily selected groups of university instructors or recent graduates. These groups apparently came in response to strong "suggestions" or thinly veiled threats that they attend; others, however, actively sought admission on a voluntary basis in order to meet the survival requirements of the new regime, or at least to learn what was expected of them in the future (GAP, 1957; Sargant, 1957).

The colleges themselves were rigidly organized and operated along communist principles of "democratic centralism." One such institution could accommodate up to 4,000 students, subdivided administratively into sections of 1,000 each, then further into classes of 100 to 200, and ultimately into six-to-ten-man discussion groups where most of the real indoctrination took place. The Head, or President, of the college was usually a noted scholar but only a figurehead in the elaborate scheme. Technically beneath him in the hierarchy were a Vice-President and the Section Leaders who were usually Communist Party members and who exerted the real authority on the central organization. Under the Section Leaders were the Class Heads, each of whom worked with three special Cadres. These Cadres, usually dedicated long-time party workers, played an important role in the thought-reform process, and they were the liaison between faculty and students. It was they, the Cadres, who did the practical, everyday work of reform.

The three Cadres in each class may be referred to according to their specific function: the *executive Cadre* was involved basically with arranging course content and programs of study; the *organizing Cadre* was most closely concerned with the structure and function of the small group and the attitudes of individual students; the *advisory Cadre,* the only one of the three who could permissibly be a woman, offered counsel and advice on personal and ideological problems that came up during the indoctrination procedure (GAP, 1957).

The Indoctrination Process

The Chairman of the Communist Party in China, Mao Tse-tung, a prolific, expressive, and able protagonist of the Party Line, was frequently referred to in discussions, and, in a highly significant speech which seems to sum up the spirit and goals of brainwashing, he stated:

> . . . . our object in exposing errors and criticizing shortcomings is like that of a doctor in curing a disease. The entire purpose is to save the person, not to cure him to death. If a man has appendicitis, the doctor performs an operation and the man is saved. If a person who commits an error, no matter how great, does not bring his disease to an incurable state by concealing it and persisting in his error, and in addition if he is genuinely and honestly willing to be cured, willing to make corrections, we will welcome him so that his disease may be cured and he can become a good comrade. It is certainly not possible to solve the problem by one flurry of blows for the sake of a moment's satisfaction. We cannot adopt a brash attitude toward diseases of thought and politics, but must have an attitude of saving men by curing their diseases. This is the correct and effective method.
>
> (GAP, 1957, p. 238)

This quotation exposes the central theme of brainwashing or thought reform as a physically nonviolent but coercive set of psychological manipulations put in the framework of a *morally right, uplifting,* and *therapeutic* experience. Brainwashing is made possible by isolating individuals from the supports and rewards of their previous milieu and then exerting group pressure upon them to adopt new, socially reinforced substitute norms. The isolation process begins with the technique of personal and social criticism.

The purpose of criticism in discussion groups was of crucial importance and was twofold: (1) it immediately discouraged any tendency toward unorthodox or nonconformist ideas or action; and (2) it served to point out the insincere, "false progressives," *i.e.,* the students who on the surface expressed entirely "correct" and conforming views but who lacked true conviction. Members of the group looked for indications of lack of real emotional involvement in others, each feeling the need to prove the reality of his own reform by making public show of personal enthusiasm and actively participating in the criticism of others. Moreover, this was an entirely acceptable way of avoiding being criticized for "failure to combine theory with practice." Everyone was made to feel guilty in varying degrees because he had, at least once in the privacy of his own thoughts, rejected one or another of the principles and precepts of communist ideology; the disconcerting part was that such thoughts seemed to show outwardly despite the conscious effort to suppress them.

As in group therapy, one was expected to receive these criticisms gratefully and graciously, viewing them as honest attempts on the parts of the critics to help correct faulty thinking. The student who was criticized was also expected, as a good group member, to anticipate, welcome, and expand on the criticisms, thus establishing the *self-criticism* process. Extensive depth analyses of one's self in minute detail was required, and this included current thoughts and behavior as well as those of the past—every experience pertaining to family, education, and intimate interpersonal relationships. The consequent insights and verbalizations were couched in the argot of communism, with its somewhat bombastic coloring.

There was a loading or biasing of the language to such a degree that terms like "liberation," "help," "progress," "the people," "proletarian," "bourgeois," and "capitalistic" became morally charged, both positively and negatively; they assumed a magical quality in and of themselves. It became difficult, using such jargon and loaded concepts, to conceive of problems in any way other than the way the Communists conceived of them. Lifton (GAP, 1957) reports that "catch phrases and semantic manipulation are so prominently developed that the student must find himself thinking and conceptualizing within their sphere." He further quotes one of his informants as follows:

> Using the same pattern of words for so long, you are so accustomed to them that you feel chained. If you make a mistake, you make a mistake within the pattern. Although you don't admit that you have adopted this kind of ideology, you are actually using it unconsciously, almost automatically. . . . At that same time I believed in certain aspects of their principles and theories, but such was the state of confusion in my own mind that I couldn't tell or make out what were the things I did believe in.
>
> (GAP, 1957, pp. 246–247)

As a natural consequence of self-criticism, the students began to *confess* within the small group to the "evils" and "transgressions" of their lives. Moral and political values became infused with each other so that thoughts and actions were negatively classified as "reactionary," or positively regarded as "progressive." The confession compulsion ran rampant through the college; everyone confessed and competed with the others to prove his frankness, thoroughness, and genuineness; there were even collective confession matches between groups. Personal confessions were the major topics at all social gatherings, small groups, informal talks with Cadres, and wall-newspaper articles. Signs were posted everywhere asking, "Have you made your full confession?" (This is frighteningly reminiscent of Orwell's "Big Brother Is Watching You!")

There were revival-like mass meetings where confession tensions were brought to a frenzied head and where a student with a particularly reprehensible background was given the opportunity to redeem himself by public confession. Hundreds or thousands of his fellow students were present when he told of his past sins which included anticommunist activities, working for the Nationalists, stealing money from his employers, and violating his neighbor's daughter or wife (all of which are crimes against the people who are the state, and thus crimes against the state).

With the passage of time, more and more "progressives" and "activists" took an aggressive leadership role, supported by the Cadres and Class Heads who were expert at manipulating the groups. If a group was not progressing, along the general plan of the thought reform, or if the group leaders were not doing their jobs well, they were replaced or re-shuffled by their superiors. The former group leader might be reduced to an ordinary student, while his group was reinforced by one or two new "activists." Despite the fact that group leaders were elected by the students, administrative shifts and transfers always insured that the position was occupied by a reliable "progressive."

Simultaneously, the student whose background was suspect or whose confessions were thought of as superficial or insincere, who was not displaying enough enthusiasm by criticizing others or whose attitudes were negativistic—the "backward elements" and "reactionaries"—was singled out for special attention. He came under doubly vehement and unswerving criticism from the group, the Cadres, and the Section Leaders, who hounded him during every waking moment to change his attitudes. Failing here, the friendly approach became threatening and he would be summoned before the Class Head to receive an official public rebuke. Finally, if everything else failed, a reactionary student was humiliated by being the subject of a massive "struggle" meeting, a ritualistic type of assembly during which he was denounced by faculty, Cadres, and comrades, and his failings publicly exposed. At this point both the student and the others attending invariably realized that failure to conform to the expectations of the college and the Communist regime literally meant no future either inside or outside of new China.

Under such intense and pervasive pressures no one could escape the resulting sense of futility, fear, and guilt. Everyone worried about the probability of surviving such an ordeal, recalling the physically violent and brutal methods used by the Communists when they first took over. Many heard stories or had personal recollections of the mass executions of anti-Communists: the public humiliation, the "bullet-in-the-back-of-the-head psychology." Very few students, indeed, wanted to earn the epithet of "reactionary."

Those who displayed emotional disorders under

these pressures were encouraged to seek counsel for their "thought problem" with advisory Cadres who framed the situation in psychotherapeutic terms in order to resolve the conflict. Psychosomatic complaints were commonly experienced in the form of gastrointestinal symptoms, aches and pains, insomnia, appetite loss, fatigue, etc. The college physician, who was invariably "reformed" or oriented in that direction, offered the psychologically appropriate reply: "There is nothing wrong with your body. It must be your thoughts that are sick. You will feel better when you have solved your problems and completed your reform" (GAP, 1957, p. 243). The painful inner tensions needed relief.

From the foregoing, though recounted in the briefest skeletal way, it seems apparent that thought reform has many features in common with the phenomenon of an induced religious conversion and a coercive form of psychotherapy, differing from these only insofar as the goals and the well-organized, consistent, co-operative scheme for achieving them are concerned. There appears to have been unanimity of thinking and action on the part of those who administered the program, from the lowest echelon to the highest, resulting in a degree of consistency and efficiency of purpose far greater than we can usually find prevailing in our own institutions of reform, *i. e.,* mental hospitals, correctional institutions, military organizations, universities, and our prisoner-of-war camps in time of war. An exception to this may be found in those religious groups or societies which have a strong, formal organization and a well-established, dedicated hierarchy, all with singleness of purpose and disciplined to obey the dictates of their ideological system rather than to display individual competitiveness or aggressive independence. These groups tend also to reinforce their members in their convictions, with the result that behavior within the group structure generally conforms to expected standards. The Communists do exactly the same—with the same consequence. As long as there are well-defined props, reinforcements, and rewards which are rigidly and consistently enforced, individuals within any system will live more or less strictly according to its precepts. Total transfer from one organized system to another seems entirely possible, especially since the individual is habituated to a *system-in-principle*. Where a person has been reared in an unorthodox, nontraditional, loosely controlled environment and is, consequently, individualistically oriented, nonconforming, and rather undisciplined from the first, it seems more difficult to habituate him to any rigid system; but it can and has been done. The experiences of American soldiers who were prisoners of war of the Chinese during the Korean War provide an excellent example of this kind of "habituation-conditioning" process. In another related context, it has been demonstrated that different ways of approaching and solving problems can be induced by consistent, programmed-type training and controlled sequential experiences so that an attitude (or *Einstellung*) can be established in most people when desired (Brownfield, 1963).

It is helpful to bear in mind that the thought reform programs taking place in China during the period between the Communist ascension to power and the beginning of the Korean War determined, in part, the approach that the Chinese would use to deal with American prisoners in Korea. There, the isolation components inherent in being far from home, family, friends, and one's own military unit were very pronounced. The atmosphere in some ways was even more conducive to thought reform than it had been within China or among unimprisoned Chinese sub-jects in the revolutionary colleges described above. The episode in Korea was far less subtle when it came to utilizing the effects of social isolation in order to make group pressures, suggestion, and overt coercion more persuasive, at least for purposes of controlling behavior. This is especially so since the focus of atten-tion was upon individuals from another racial and cultural group, which meant that personal identifica-tion with the captors as "friendly" was a bit more difficult to achieve than was the case when Chinese were reforming Chinese.

CHAPTER 4 ⫸

Brainwashing in Korea

Methods of ideological reform such as those outlined here seem to be most effective when the whole culture reinforces their goals. The Chinese intellectuals who were exposed to the indoctrination program of the revolutionary college had to remain in the Chinese Communist culture which consistently rewarded and punished and thus perpetuated the work of the thought reform. The Western world, on the other hand, creates different kinds of demands for the Westerner, demands that are perhaps more contradictory and inconsistent because of the lack of a well-defined totalitarian structure, but still requiring a modicum of behavioral conformity. Our culture may not so readily support the goals of our own vehicles of attitudinal and behavioral change, *i.e.*, psychotherapy, correctional rehabilitation, and other remedial techniques. While the degree of success attending the Chinese thought reform process may be difficult to assess, we have at least some insight into how the Communists were able to entrench themselves so well in China, and perhaps a partial answer as to how they became so well established in other countries. It now becomes somewhat easier to understand and recognize the philosophy of thought reform and the lenient policy, and to see how these were effectively applied to American prisoners of war in the Korean War.

Divergent Viewpoints

Several theories have been advanced to explain why
it is that the techniques of ideological reform, as observed during the Chinese Communist exploitation of
United Nations prisoners of war in North Korea, met
with such seeming success. One viewpoint alleges that
methods of manipulating behavior have been developed to such a degree that a person's will to resist is
broken and he cannot help but respond in much the
same way as animals do in conditioned-reflex experiments along Pavlovian lines (Brozek, 1950, 1955;
Huxley, 1958; Mayo, 1953; Meerloo, 1951, 1952, 1953,
1954, 1955, 1956; Olds, 1955, 1958; Sargant, 1957;
Skinner, 1956; Tennien, 1952), *i.e.,* automatically, un-
consciously, and unwillingly. Many writers have correlated the compliance and submissiveness effected by
the Communists in their prisoners with similar phenomena observed in the laboratory, *e.g.,* experiments
with hypnogogic and hallucinogenic drugs, hypnosis,
sleeplessness and sensory deprivation, semistarvation,
electrical stimulation of the brain, and the social and
psychological effects of group pressures toward conformity (Bexton, 1953; Bexton, Heron, and Scott,
1954; Farber, Harlow, and West, 1957; GAP, 1956,
1957; Haring, 1957; Heron, Bexton, and Hebb, 1953;
Heron, Doane, and Scott, 1956; Hunter, 1953; Janis,
1949; Jordan, 1957; Lilly, Hughes, Alvord, and Galkin, 1955; Mayo, 1953; Penfield and Rasmussen, 1950;
Rolin, 1956; Scott, Bexton, Heron, and Doane, 1959;
Silverman, Cohen, Shmavonian, and Greenberg, 1961;
Winokur, 1955; Kiskind, 1958). Others, more conservative, have challenged this somewhat extreme position. While granting that brainwashing may be a
powerful coercive process, particularly among those
who are unaware that it is taking place, they have

been impressed by the strength, resilience, and stability of long-standing values and social controls, and by the individual's rational regard for himself either as limiting the efficacy of attempts to change his thinking, or as enabling the victim to resist brainwashing entirely (Bauer, 1957; Biderman, 1956, 1957a, 1959; Federn, 1951; Hacker, 1955; Hinkle and Wolff, 1956; Riesman, 1952; Schaffer, 1954; Schein, 1957a, 1957b; Sykes, 1956; West, 1957; Wolff, 1959).

On the other hand, certain observers have attributed the Communists' more apparent than real successes to individual defects of character, personality, stamina, and moral fiber in those who collaborated; or to a general deterioration of vitality, social responsibility, values, and controls in contemporary but decadent Western society (Haring, 1957; Kinkead, 1959; Mayer, 1956; Thorin, 1956; U.S. Congress, 1956, 1957; U.S. Department of the Army, 1956). In the same vein, disputes regarding the extent to which repatriated prisoners of war are legally and morally responsible for their compromising behavior under the stresses of the indoctrination program, especially when they have yielded information or made "confessions," becloud the real issues with emotional and often unrealistic, moralistic, and inappropriate philosophical considerations (Biderman and Monroe, 1958; Kinkead, 1957, 1959; Miller, 1957; *Columbia Law Review*, 1956; Murray, 1955; Peterson, 1953; Prugh, 1955; Schein, 1957b; U.S. Department of Defense, 1955).

General Predisposition

The situation that developed in Korea in 1950 caught most Americans (and other involved Western nations) largely off guard. The primarily regular army troops who fought the initial actions were poorly prepared, physically and psychologically, to cope with the unexpected and rather unorthodox methods of warfare they experienced (Schein, 1962). Because of preconceptions about the brutality and cruelty of Orientals, based largely on experiences with the Japanese in World War II, soldiers who fell prisoner to the North Koreans in the initial phase of the conflict half expected the atrocities and abuses that were meted out; they were thoroughly incensed and quite convinced that they would not survive captivity. (The North Koreans did, at first, "execute" many G.I.'s as "war criminals" upon capture.) They were even less prepared for the lack of such treatment and the completely different approach employed when the Chinese "People's Volunteers" entered the fighting.

In addition, the men were not clearly aware of what they were fighting for or why, or even what kind of enemy they were facing. When the Chinese came into the war they penetrated deeply into rear areas and captured many men completely by surprise; it was generally felt by those who were overtaken in this way that their leadership left much to be desired and that communication was quite poor. There was also a widespread predisposition to blame the United Nations command for their being captured, thus creating the distorted impression that they had somehow been betrayed.

Physical Conditions

The majority of men were captured in Korea in the fall and winter of 1950. This necessitated long forced marches to temporary prison camps and collecting points under painfully uncomfortable weather conditions, the chief nemesis being freezing cold. The men were physically exhausted, had no adequate medical treatment, ate an unfamiliar diet (which they frequently vomited), and suffered from severe frostbite; the combination of these conditions resulted in an exceptionally high death rate that winter (about 38 percent mortality). The North Koreans, who were extremely brutal, and later the Chinese, who were less brutal, claimed that their supply shortages were the result of United Nations bombings of supply lines; thus there was little food and practically no medicine. This kind of explanation made it difficult to hate the captors because, after all, the poor conditions might not have been intentional on their part.

As mentioned, the North Koreans were rather vicious in their treatment; they often shot captives, or, if they decided to allow them to live, beat them mercilessly, exposed them to tortures and indignities beyond description, and generally facilitated the desired impression that to be taken prisoner was tantamount to a death sentence. Soon after the war began, however, the Chinese took over the operation of prisoner-of-war camps and collecting points, so that the bedraggled and confused captives found themselves being handed over by their cruel North Korean captors to relatively friendly and "humanitarian" Chinese.

The tactic of presenting themselves as friendly was evidently an extension of the *lenient policy* and had the effect of surprising and shocking the prisoners who had really expected to be killed. It made them feel somewhat grateful to the Chinese to have been delivered from the abusive North Koreans as well as from the battlefield; or it made some feel guilty for not being grateful to the enemy who *seemed* to be fair and understanding. The lenient policy was explained to groups of prisoners shortly after capture; they were told that because the United Nations had entered the war illegally, it was an aggressor and all U.N. military personnel were actually "criminals"—they could be shot summarily, as the North Koreans at first had done. But since the average soldier was only carrying out orders, it was his leaders who were the real criminals, and the soldier was only a dupe or tool. Thus Chinese soldiers would regard all prisoners of war as "students" rather than prisoners, and would teach them the real facts and "truth" about this war. Those who refused to co-operate by attending school and voluntarily learning, could always revert back to the status of "war criminal" and be shot.

For weeks following their capture, the men were marshaled at collecting points in large groups and marched northward. As already pointed out, the stresses of these forced marches were acute and the Chinese set a severe pace that displayed little consideration for the fatigue that resulted from the physical exertion, the unattended wounds, sickness, diarrhea, and frostbite. Those who could not keep pace were abandoned to die alone (not killed by the Chinese directly) unless they could be assisted by their fellow prisoners who were most likely equally debilitated. Marching only at night and keeping under cover in daylight, the harried prisoners were made to fear bombing and strafing attacks by their own United Nations Command planes. The idea of being killed by bullets or bombs from one's own side certainly did nothing to maintain firm and effective ties between the prisoners of war and the United Nations forces, especially when the Chinese seemed to be showing more concern for their prisoners' safety than the Americans were.

Psychological Conditions

Schein (1962, p. 255) describes the psychological situation of these conditions as a "chronic cycle of fear, relief, and new fear." The prisoners were fearful of dying, or that they might never be repatriated, or that they would never have a chance to communicate with the outside again, or that no one even knew they were alive. On the other hand, it was the Chinese who tried to reassure them and promised repatriation just as soon as possible; it was the "enemy" who told them that conditions would be improved (and the Chinese did improve them somewhat) and that they could contact the outside as soon as the situation allowed. In their *manner* and their *words* the Chinese were generally solicitous and sympathetic. The isolation from a familiar environment, however, was awesome.

Disorganization of the formal authority structure among the prisoners was also achieved by the simple device of segregating the commissioned and noncommissioned officers, and by using low-ranking and collaborating prisoners as squad leaders or for other administrative leadership positions. Sometimes a Chinese would be placed in the squad leader's position too. Group gatherings and activities not consistent with the political objectives of the Communists were forbidden and all natural leaders who sprang up spontaneously to organize groups were removed from the area and transferred to "Reactionary Camps" where the treatment was somewhat harsher. After all the formal and natural leaders were removed (accounting for about 5 percent of the prisoner population), the remaining prisoners were almost totally under the physical and psychological control of the Chinese. Lines of authority, now successfully broken, group cohesiveness, and morale suffered equally; if one was competitive with others for the necessities, it was difficult to maintain close ties. The men's illnesses repelled one another too; diarrhea and incontinence were endemic and it was not pleasant to live in over-crowded huts with those so afflicted.

A small number of prisoners attempted to escape but were recaptured shortly and returned to the camp. No one was usually punished for this either; the procedure was to take the attempted escapee aside (an English-speaking Chinese did this) and chide him with some condescending tolerance, pointing out the terrible chance he had taken of getting killed and demonstrating how foolish escape was when he was safer in the camp than back on the front lines! This method, combined with other subtle techniques of group control, resulted in the almost incredible fact that not once during the entire Korean episode did a prisoner succeed in permanently escaping from any of the camps set up by the Chinese. Some escaped near the time of capture or at collecting points, but once having reached a permanent camp, no one ever escaped for good. As few as five or six guards armed only with rifles guarded as many as 500 prisoners; there were no machine-gun towers, barbed-wire complexes, guard dogs, or other devices normally used to control large groups of captives. Yet no one escaped (Mayer, 1956).

The Chinese further fostered low morale and a sense of isolation and abandonment by allowing only collection notices, divorce subpoenas, "Dear John" letters, and other demoralizing mail to go through their unique censorship system which held back "good" letters and let the "bad" ones through. They also systematically reported false or misleading news about United Nations defeats and losses, showed stock market gains in the *Wall Street Journal* correlated with the advent and duration of the war, filled camp libraries with communist literature, etc.

Later they conducted "courses" in American history that denounced some "evils" of the capitalistic system and glorified the solutions to those evils offered by communism. They even taught soldiers to read and write who had not been able to do so before, at or above the fourth-grade level, thus proving themselves to be "benevolent benefactors" and further destroying the ties with home. In short, the whole environment was designed to support and reinforce positive, favorable responses toward communist ideology and extinguish negative, procapitalistic attitudes simply by not giving them the credit of attention. They did *not* attempt to make Communists of the prisoners, but merely to develop sympathies for communism, *e.g.*, "It'll never work in America—we're too rich; but what a wonderful thing for China!"

The Organized "Program"

The whole process of brainwashing in Korea can best be conceived of in two phases. The first phase lasted anywhere from one to six months after capture (depending on time of initial capture) and included the forced marches to North Korea and the debilitating conditions of the temporary camps. This was something of a "softening up" period. In these camps, the hardships of wounds, fatigue, disease, and exposure took a heavy toll in lives—higher than at any time in the history of any Americans in captivity since the Revolutionary War (Mayer, 1956; Mayo, 1953). Approximately 38 percent of the prisoners died during this period. However, it was felt by many, including some physicians who themselves were prisoners and survived, that a good many of these deaths could not be accounted for by the presence of a physical disease.

It appeared that most of these men had become so apathetic under stress that they stopped caring about their physical needs, withdrew further into themselves, declined the little food they had, refused to exercise, and lay down in a corner, curled up into a ball and died! Eyewitness accounts emphasized that the men were sane, though rather passive, dependent, and anxious, but seemed to give up and accept death as an alternative to the frustrations and deprivations of the environment (GAP, 1957, p. 256).

A prisoner who was close to this "apathy death" might be saved by one or both of two things: forcing him to his feet and getting him to do something—anything—and/or arousing his anger or concern about a current or future problem. "In one such case," Schein relates (GAP, 1957, p.256), "*therapy* consisted of kicking a man until he was mad enough to get up and fight." All the while, the North Koreans played the role of the villainous "bogeymen" who were held in check by the benevolent Chinese, who in turn were handicapped in giving "better" treatment because the captives' own Air Forces were harassing supply lines. Moreover, they subtly implied that if the prisoners would take a more "co-operative attitude" (if they would support the "propaganda for peace" program), conditions could be better. The suggestion here was that the prisoners of war themselves were responsible for their own uncomfortable conditions.

The second phase lasted two or more years and began with the arrival at a permanent camp where some relief from the physical hardships was evident. Food, medicine, and shelter, while far from plentiful or adequate, were better than in the temporary camps and could sustain life and health to a degree. There was a natural tendency on the captives' part to feel grateful to the Chinese for "rescuing" them from oblivion and abuse under the North Koreans in the temporary camps. Under these conditions the Chinese radically increased their indoctrination efforts to undermine loyalties to the political, social, and economic systems of the United States and the West, and to involve the prisoners in the Communist propaganda machine.

The program was an integral part of the total camp routine; it had broad and inclusive aims, like controlling a large group with a small staff of guards, inculcating the prisoners with communist ideology, interrogation for intelligence information, obtaining "confessions" for propaganda uses, developing a core of informers and collaborators for both spying and propaganda purposes, and "educating" the prisoners to their "truths" about the war, as well as teaching illiterates and near-illiterates the necessary language skills they did not get under capitalism. The entire social milieu had to be manipulated, and most of the success the Chinese had in achieving their goals resulted from their *total control* of the environment. They did not use any one technique in particular, and certainly not intentional sensory deprivation or perceptual isolation, though solitary confinement was resorted to frequently.

Men were segregated by race, nationality, and rank, which allowed the opportunity to play on racial discord, national rivalries, and rank consciousness as evils of the capitalist system. While the Chinese placed their own men in charge of platoons and companies, the selection of prisoner-of-war squad leaders was usually made from the lowest ranks, thus reminding the prisoners that the old status-rank system was no longer meaningful. No group meetings, such as religious services, were allowed, and the Communists systematically played men against each other. Particularly effective was the practice of getting information about someone's activities from informers or spies, no matter how trivial, and then calling that person in for questioning about this. If a man resisted giving information, he would be shown a signed confession by a fellow prisoner disclosing the same information they had been asking for. The prisoners became so conditioned to the idea that the Communists knew everything they wanted to know before an interrogation session, that they resisted giving such information less and less; ultimately they gave information that the Communists did not know beforehand, but the unwitting prisoner was unaware of this.

Another device was to make those who were not collaborators appear as if they were, by suddenly bestowing special and elaborate favors upon them in a most conspicuous way. Such methods helped create the impression that the prisoners' ranks were infiltrated by spies and informers and thus no one could be trusted. The men retreated further into themselves and could not get together even for purposes of resisting or planning an escape. Everyone around them *seemed* to be co-operating with the Communists and the tendency began to be to acquiesce to the seeming pressures from within the group to do the same.

The sense of social isolation was further intensified by complete control of information media in the camps, where only communist newspapers, magazines, books, radio, and movies were permitted. The clever mail-sorting censorship, the lack of support from others in maintaining old attitudes and ties, the vilification of "imperialistic" Western capitalism, the actual physical and emotional isolation from communication with family, friends and countrymen—all contributed further to the overwhelming feeling of loneliness, frustration, and dependence upon the Chinese.

It was the Chinese who offered to fill these gaps with meaningful social relationships, through the sharing of common beliefs and activities like "peace committees," which required agreement with the Communists if one wished to participate simply for the sheer stimulation of activity. Chinese interrogators or "instructors" actually befriended the men, offering them close personal relations, living and eating with the prisoners for long periods, and giving them encouragement and hope for the future—all with a communist slant.

The systematic manipulation of the environment also included rewards and punishments such as extra food, medicine, privileges, and recognition; whereas threats of death, nonrepatriation, withholding of food and medicines, reprisals against families back home, and imprisonment or solitary confinement were used as deterrents to resistance. Despite these threats, which were always in the prisoners' minds, the only actual punishment consistently employed was imprisonment and solitary confinement.

The over-all effect was to produce three distinct categories of prisoners, characterized by the degree to which they were perceived by themselves and others as collaborating with their captors. "Progressives" were those prisoners who were regarded by the Communists and other prisoners of war as receptive to the indoctrination, co-operative to its expectations, and ideologically sympathetic to the cause—often participating in the propaganda efforts and attempting to convince others of the "rightness" of their (communistic) position. "Reactionaries" were prisoners who were not good "students," resisted indoctrination, maintained a hostile and refractory attitude toward the Chinese and communism, actively organized resistance, and led rebellious discussions in the criticism group; these were quickly removed as soon as they were identified and after more stringent methods had failed to change them.

The largest group, by far, were the "Neutrals" who "played it cool," or otherwise tried not to provoke the Chinese against them, doing only what was necessary to maintain reasonably peaceful relations without committing themselves to one extreme or the other. In essence, each camp (except the Reactionary camp) was basically composed of Progressives and Neutrals—a climate quite favorable by default for thought reform goals since there was no prevailing active or negative resistance.

Collaboration

In this setting, and under the tremendous pressure which the Chinese put on the men to make radio broadcasts, films, tape recordings and to sign peace petitions and confessions, some ten to fifteen percent of the men began collaborating, not because they were morally deficient (there may have been some), not because they were disloyal (this might have applied to a few), and not because they believed in the communist ideology (some did), but simply because there were no other standards of behavior—or frame of reference—by which they could perceive their own actions as being somehow not acceptable to those who later judged them to be wrong. Loss of group support meant that there was no way of confirming or checking alternative ways of behaving, and thus many made obvious errors in judgment; they could not anticipate the consequences of what they had done (GAP, 1957,

p. 258). This does not imply, however, that the Chinese had a great deal of success in permanently changing attitudes and beliefs; once the prisoners returned to the environment which again supported old, more deeply-ingrained beliefs (that milieu in which they grew up and first learned how to believe), the work of the brainwashing became undone. It is true that doubt and confusion were elicited among the prisoners because they had to examine, perhaps for the first time, their own way of thinking, but remarkably few changes actually occurred that resembled true *conversion* to communism. Prisoners who occupied a low status position in our society were more prone to *sympathize* with communism, mainly because they had not been adequately informed through education and experience, and the principles of democracy were not very real or meaningful to them. Schein (1956, 1957a, 1957b, 1959, 1960a, 1960b, 1961, 1962), who summarized the motives for collaboration, and qualified his effort by saying that it was impossible to determine how many cases of each type or motive there may have been, lists the following:

(1) Some men collaborated for outright opportunistic reasons: these men lacked any kind of stable group identification and exploited the situation for its material benefits without regard for the consequences to themselves, their fellow prisoners, or their country.

(2) Some men collaborated because their egos were too weak to withstand the physical and psychological rigors; these men were primarily motivated by fear, though they often rationalized their behavior; they were unable to resist any kind of authority figure, and were highly susceptible to being blackmailed once they had begun to collaborate.

(3) Some men collaborated with the firm conviction that they were infiltrating the Chinese ranks and obtaining in-

telligence information which would be useful to the Army. This was a convenient rationalization for anyone who could not withstand the pressures. Many of these men were initially tricked into collaboration or were motivated by a desire to communicate with the outside world. None of the types mentioned thus far became ideologically confused; what communist beliefs they might have professed were for the benefit of the Chinese only.

(4) The prisoner who was vulnerable to the *ideological* appeal because of his low status in this society, often collaborated with the conviction that he was doing the right thing in supporting the communist peace movement. This group included the younger and less intelligent men from backward or rural areas, the malcontents, and members of various minority groups. These men often viewed themselves as failures in our society and felt that society had never given them a chance. They were positively attracted by the immediate status and privileges that went with being a "progressive," and by the promise of important roles which they could presumably play in the peace movement of the future.*

Air Force Prisoners of the Chinese Communists

It should be mentioned that Air Force personnel who became prisoners of war of the Chinese Communists and the North Koreans were handled somewhat differently from ground force prisoners, although most of the influences discussed above were present in their indoctrination. These people were far less prepared for the unique conditions of captivity into which they literally "fell," and there were a number of qualitative differences which determined the differential treatment (GAP, 1957; West, 1957, 1958).

1. Airmen had no close contact with the enemy or

* This section appeared in Symposium No. 4, published by the Group for the Advancement of Psychiatry and entitled *Methods of Forceful Indoctrination: Observations and Interviews*, pp. 259-260. Used by permission of GAP and the author.

his terrain prior to being captured. They usually went abruptly from relatively comfortable conditions to prisoner status.

2. Most Air Force prisoners suffered some injury as a result of crashes or otherwise getting to the ground.

3. Flyers were generally of higher rank than ground force prisoners; 70 percent were officers.

4. The Air Force prisoner of war was generally more knowledgeable than his ground force counterparts since he had usually been getting a better perspective of the war situation back at the base.

5. There was a higher degree of specialized technical training among Air Force prisoners; they had more useful intelligence information with a high priority than did ordinary "dog faces" or "ground pounders."

6. The average airman had a better educational level and was thus better informed than the other types of prisoners; 53 percent of the Air Force prisoners had some college training as compared with only 5 percent of the ground forces.

7. Because of their superior rank, technical skills, educational level, and better initial physical health (even though injured), most air personnel were almost automatically "reactionaries," *i.e.*, more resistive to the indoctrination methods used in the other camps.

With obvious recognition of these differences, the Chinese looked upon captured airmen in a special way. American and United Nations aircraft had flown over enemy lines almost unopposed, at first, and both Communist military and civilian personnel were cognizant of the great damage done by Air Force operations. Starting February 21, 1952, the Communist international "germ-warfare" propaganda program was begun, and the most obvious "blame" was placed on the flyers, who would presumably be the instruments of delivery of bacteriological weapons.

Air Force prisoners were thus considered especially valuable for propaganda purposes as well as sources of good intelligence information. Because of these and the other differences mentioned, the Communists used more stringent and unusual methods. They did not segregate Air Force officers and enlisted men, but considered both as an integral group. They used the technique of physical isolation or solitary confinement for long periods with individuals, exerting more pressures and physical coercion in order to obtain false confessions and technical information. Air Force personnel were punitively subjected to greater humiliations and indignities but offered the same rewards for co-operation that ground forces had been given, including being placed back in a communal compound with other prisoners. The Chinese attempted to get captives to participate in indoctrination "classes" and "lectures" in order to get them to sympathize with communist principles.

In general, the efforts of the Chinese to elicit collaboration or to indoctrinate Air Force personnel met with much *less* success than their efforts with ground force personnel. The different results may be attributable to the qualitative differences mentioned as well as to the differential treatment accorded airmen. There was, however, more success in eliciting intelligence information, but this appears to have been done in a rather conventional way, *i.e.,* threat of death, torture, psychological abuses, and strict interrogatory techniques. A few Air Force personnel died as a direct result of attempts to coerce information or because of their refusal to co-operate; some died as a result of untreated injuries, others because of torture or "execution" as "war criminals." They were, all in all, treated badly and had less difficulty mustering their hatred against the enemy.

Implications

The major stresses of isolation and confinement in a North Korean prisoner-of-war camp under the Chinese have been related here, and the responses to these stresses have been outlined, though not in great detail. Collaboration perhaps can best be conceived of as an effect of clever and systematically created social isolation and group disorganization, where the environment consistently rewarded those responses termed "collaboration," and extinguished those which were not consistent with the goals of brainwashing. Such group disorganization and isolation hindered the development of an adequate frame of reference, consensual validation, co-operative group resistance, or the insights necessary to understand and handle those prisoners who may have been initially duped into some act of collaboration, or who showed poor judgment. Any ideological involvement appeared to be the product of some predisposition associated with a low status position in our society; the conditions of social isolation, with its concomitant stresses, served to intensify the expression of such predispositions.

In order to produce behavior inconsistent with an individual's prior standards and values, the Chinese first disorganized and isolated the group and thus removed the supports from those prior standards; then they substituted new ones (as in the revolutionary college). Emotional supports and ties with home were also undermined, but the Chinese also provided substitutes via personal friendships with "instructors" or interrogators and a simple reward-punishment system based on approval-disapproval. The prisoner was thus placed in a unique, ambiguous situation and left to find the appropriate standards of conduct for himself; through simple trial and error, he slowly discerned which behavior was rewarded and which was not. The same pressures seen in the thought reform program within China also operated on the prisoners in Korea.

Part 2 ‹‹‹‹‹‹

The Scientific Approach:
Experimental Isolation

We live by day, in a sheltered physical world,
but also most of the time in a
sheltered psychological world consisting of
the ordered behavior of our fellows.
What we call "civilization" is a kind of
behavioral cocoon which fosters the illusion
that civilized man is by nature calm,
dispassionate, and logical. This is illusion only,
but on it rest most of our discussions of how
to deal with the great social problems...

—*Donald O. Hebb*

CHAPTER 5

Neurological, Developmental, and Other Considerations

Brief mention can profitably be made of some of the neuropsychological correlates of observed isolation effects, more specifically those arising from the experimental reduction or elimination of sensory stimulation for individuals in sensory deprivation. Details of the experimental work will be dealt with in other chapters; it should be kept in mind here, however, that sensory deprivation and social isolation are qualitatively different, though there are many similarities. In *sensory deprivation* (or *perceptual isolation*) we have a situation in which normal sensory stimulation or input is greatly reduced, eliminated, or made invariant and monotonous; *social isolation* entails only the elimination or reduction of communication through the senses of one individual or group with other individuals or groups. Both situations can induce stress, depending upon the way in which they are viewed. When the senses are deprived, there is inherently and automatically a component of social isolation. This is not always so in social isolation where the senses are not necessarily deprived and the person retains full sensory capacity while unable to communicate or receive communication from others (*e.g.*, consensual validation, information, social gratification). For the moment let us first be concerned with deprivation of ordinary stimulation through the sense organs to the brain; later, this will allow us to understand better the more complex situation of social isolation, which was one of the primary features of brainwashing and the anecdotal isolation experiences discussed in the preceding chapters.

Neuropsychological Evidence

Research has suggested that the natural response of the brain stem reticular system, located roughly at the base of the skull, to repeated or monotonous sensory stimulation, is a rapid adaptation and consequent extinguishing of arousal or attention-directing functions until a novel stimulus representing a change in intensity, frequency, or shift to another sense modality is introduced (Jasper, 1958). As in the previously given example of the soldiers who can sleep during a continual barrage, but who awaken because the noise stops, this represents a change in the intensity and frequency of the stimulus and causes arousal. It is not so much the stimulation itself as it is the *change* in the stimulation that causes attention to be focused. We live in a continually changing stimulus world, and the focus of attention, while continually changing too, can only be maintained as long as such variation occurs. If there is little or no variation, such as in monotonous or boring situations, attention will lapse and we can fall into the trancelike states reported by the polar isolates, the Eskimos, and others who have found themselves in an environment of static changelessness (*cf.* Chapter 2). This appears to be a fundamental principle of behavior in all living organisms with a brain and a nervous system. The actual mechanisms and pathways through the reticular system are not yet known, and nothing specific has been discovered about the way in which stimuli are "processed" in this part of the brain. If such nonspecific influences are involved in this effect, they may provide a means by which the brain is able to exclude irrelevant incoming information during the focus of attention (Hernandez-Peon, Scherrer and Jouvet, 1956). In fact, the identification of other nonspecific neural mechanisms lying between *sensory* (incoming) and *motor* (outgoing) processes in the brain has helped us to understand more about how the nervous system is organized (Magoun, 1958). We now know that the reciprocal ascending and descending connections between points in the brain stem and wide areas of the cerebral hemispheres, including the cortex, are involved in arousal to wakefulness and alerting to attention (Magoun, 1952).

Researchers (French, 1957; Moruzzi and Magoun, 1949) have thus identified an area in the brain stem reticular formation which reacts in the same nonspecific way to all incoming stimulation from different sense receptors, *i.e.,* eyes, nose, ears, skin, etc. This response is simply to arouse the brain, rather than to relay any specific message; its signals are projected to the entire cortex rather than to any one particular association center in the brain. This *reticular activating system,* or RAS as it has been called (French, 1957; Magoun, 1952), is selective to specific stimuli in that it makes differential responses to sudden or even continual sensory input, as if it had the ability to discriminate between different kinds of stimulation (in terms of quality). If the RAS does not function normally, as when there is actual physical damage to that part of the brain, a state of consciousness becomes impossible; the undamaged system, however, can maintain a wakeful state even if the cerebral cortex is absent. Decorticate animals, and even humans who through accident have lost large areas of cortex, still show signs of being awake and responsive to their environment. Here, "wakefulness" is not synonymous with "consciousness" in its usually understood definition, since it is possible to be awake yet be conscious of nothing (at least externally) as is a newborn infant, a hypnotic subject, or presumably a person in a special isolation chamber in which there may be almost nothing to perceive and discriminate and thus nothing to which to respond. Under these conditions internal events may or may not become focused upon.

In other words, while a stimulus evokes or guides a specific bit of behavior, it also serves the nonspecific purpose of maintaining a normal state of arousal through the RAS. In conditions of stimulus impoverishment, decreased variation, or extreme reduction, the neural impulses of sensation which normally traverse through and activate the reticular system, are also nonexistent or markedly reduced in intensity, frequency, and duration. This produces an effect similar to that which happens when there is disease, injury, or blockage of the brain stem; this is called *deafferentiation*—the removal of incoming stimulation. Since actual damage or blockage makes it impossible to study the consequent effects on mental processes like thinking, perception, and imagination, because the person with such a condition would usually be sick, unconscious, or dead, the methods of experimentally controlling the approximate input of stimulation by the isolation procedures, which will be discussed later, make it possible to study the effects on live, responsive, healthy human beings. Besides, as one group of researchers (Bexton, Heron and Scott, 1954) has so poignantly observed, people are understandably reluctant to have their brain stems cut, even for the sake of science!

Other neurological and physiological concomitants have been reported under conditions of sensory and perceptual isolation, the major features of which will be discussed in the chapters on experimental isolation procedures and their results. Modification or alteration of sensory input appears to produce concurrent modification and alteration of response or output, so that changes in subjective experience are frequently reported.

The qualitative characteristics of cognitive performance tasks are also sometimes observably different; they are objectively better or worse, depending upon the particular function being tested (Brownfield, 1964a). Changes in hormonal secretion rates and electroencephalographic wave patterns, galvanic skin resistance, sleep-wakefulness ratios, caloric utilization, differential reaction times, liminal (threshold) discriminations, body temperature, and other neurophysiological processes have also been correlated with the psychological conditions imposed by sensory-perceptual limitation (Fiske and Maddi, 1961; Solomon *et al.*, 1961; Biderman and Zimmer, 1961; Vernon, 1963). The significance and meaning of these observed changes have not yet been fully understood, but research efforts are continually addressing themselves to this problem and answers are—we hope—forthcoming.

Early Experience

At this point it should be apparent that human beings are individually, socially, and physiologically dependent not only upon stimulation *per se*, but upon a continually varied and changing sensory stimulation in order to maintain normal, intelligent, co-ordinated, adaptive behavior and mental functioning. Turning now to early experience, professional literature abounds with reports of experimental studies designed to investigate the deleterious effects of early environmental conditions of deprivation on later behavior (King, 1958). Most of this work has been done with animals, mainly because of the obvious advantages involved in studying organisms whose rate of maturational development is relatively faster than that of human beings. Attempts at human studies are, for the most part, necessarily restricted to observational methods, case histories, and other types of *ex post facto* designs because of the difficulties inherent in controlling the conditions of early experience or of manipulating the environment (Davis, 1940; Dennis and Dennis, 1940; Hill and Robinson, 1929; Melzack, 1954; Spitz, 1954, 1955; and others). Generally, however, most experimental efforts with animals or observational methods with humans involve the impoverishment or enrichment of stimulation at various developmental stages in order to assess the later differential effects of such treatment. It is important to note the emphasis placed upon the imposition of the conditions at a stage in the organism's development when it has not fully matured. On the other hand, sensory deprivation research is usually concerned primarily with the fully matured adult's current response to stimulus reduction, decreased variation, or absence of stimulus input. In many respects, the results of early experience studies and sensory deprivation research are comparable, *i.e.*, the cognitive, perceptual and motivational changes reported are similar, though not precisely the same.

Among the earlier observations along these lines (although there were many studies of a similar nature in the early 1940's) to which this finding has added greater understanding, are the reports by Spitz (Spitz, 1954, 1955) of a phenomenon in infants he called *hospitalism*. Infants in a foundling nursery who were not handled or stimulated often, who received minimal care but were not exposed to fondling, cuddling, and physical and emotional contacts with their mothers, showed deleterious behavioral and developmental effects. The mortality rate among these babies was exceptionally high—close to 100 percent—though disease was not a primary factor. The report suggests that the conditions of social isolation and maternal deprivation were causative, contributing to the deaths of some, and perhaps to subsequent intellectual and emotional defects among those few who survived. While these devastating consequences may be attributed wholly or partially to the social deprivation in the infants' environment, there is also more recent evidence suggesting that a degree of sensory deprivation, particularly *tactuo-kinesthetic* (touch-movement) restriction, may be more directly responsible.

Harlow (1953, 1958, 1962; Harlow and Zimmer, 1954) investigated the hypothesis that infants raised without the opportunity to receive early tactual and kinesthetic stimulation through physical contact with the mother later displayed personality maladjustment although they were breast-fed; this was originally advanced to refute the Freudian theory which suggested that frustration of infantile oral needs accounted for later personality difficulties and a hostile, dependent orientation toward the world. Working with monkeys, because they were readily available and easily subjected to environmental manipulation, Harlow raised two groups of individual babies differently: in one group he provided the infants with a soft, terry-cloth mother-surrogate doll figure which contained a nursing bottle in its chest; while for the other group, the mother-surrogate was a hard, wire-mesh figure also fitted with the nursing bottle. The difference between the two was only in the tactile qualities of the food source, and the differential behavioral characteristics of the two groups, if such appeared, could be attributed to the tactuo-kinesthetic variable. This, in fact, was what Harlow generally found: monkeys raised with the soft, terry-cloth mother-surrogate developed an attachment to the figure and displayed normal, playful, friendly monkey behavior, while those raised with the hard, wire mother generally became skittish, hyperactive, irascible, disorganized, and maladaptive. Harlow described some of the latter group as merely passing long hours sitting and rocking autistically, much as childhood schizophrenics do; and their responses to novel stimulation appeared to be hostile, fearful, disorganized, and not consistent with what one normally expects from monkeys. Besides social isolation, it would appear that those sensory modes associated with *cutaneous* (skin), *tactual* (touch), *kinesthetic* (movement), and subsequent bodily stimulation are also rather important variables in the development of the organism and are necessary for the establishment and maintenance of normal, intelligent, organized behavior. Without such stimulation it is doubtful that survival would be insured, as in the case of Spitz's infant group, which had a very low survival rate, and in Harlow's monkeys, which probably could not survive without the humane care given in the laboratory. A specific type of cutaneous, tactual, and kinesthetic sensory deprivation thus seems to account for the deleterious results observed.

In man, it was commonly thought that the visual field predominated. Indeed it is quite important; but the kinds of research evidence arising from studies like those cited above, and from recent experimental sensory deprivation investigations, seem to suggest that either there is more reliance on interaction between sensory modes than previously thought, or that cutaneous, tactual, and kinesthetic sensations play a more primary and determining role than was hitherto credited. Helen Keller, for example, developed a very adequate sense of self-awareness and abstract cognitive ability without vision and hearing, receiving information of her existence as well as of others only through her tactile, kinesthetic, thermal, gustatory, and olfactory senses.*

Animals exposed to varying conditions of deprivation, restriction, or isolation at different chronological ages may manifest entirely different behavioral responses depending upon the particular developmental stage at which they undergo the treatment (King, 1958; Riesen, 1947, 1961a, 1961b). In sensory deprivation research, the organism's ability or inability to adapt to the stresses of the contemporary stimulus situation or to no stimulation at all is of primary concern; and reports of the consequences of such stresses display a good deal of uniformity, depending of course upon the type of deprivation employed. Whereas early deprivation almost always appears to result in permanent and usually deleterious alteration of typical species behavior, sensory or perceptual impoverishment or invariability seems to have its greatest effect upon the mature organism at the time it is being subjected to these conditions. Persistence of

* One wonders what would happen if a person could see and hear but not feel any bodily sensations. Experiments with the drug Sernyl (see later chapter), which does produce tactuo-kinesthetic sensory anaesthesia while leaving vision and audition intact, suggests that cognitive disorientation, disorganization, and hallucinations, among other deteriorative effects, do occur.

effects varies with the intensity and duration of the isolation, as well as with the individual subject; but no permanent, lasting changes have ever been reliably and consistently reported in the mature subject. As yet, persistence of effects in experimental isolation is known to last at most six weeks (Bexton, Heron and Scott, 1954), but is more frequently reported to last only a matter of hours or days (Arnhoff, Leon, and Brownfield, 1962; Cohen, Silverman, Bressler, and Shmavonian, 1958; Davis, 1940; Lilly, 1956; Lilly and Shurley, 1958; Mendelson and Foley, 1956; Solomon *et al.*, 1961).

Feral Man and Cases of Extreme Isolation in Humans

The term "feral" (wild) man is applied to extreme cases of human isolation (*cf.* Zingg, 1940) in which infants allegedly have been abandoned and later adopted and suckled by wild animals, or older children have wandered away into the wilds and somehow survived on their own without further human assistance or contact. Not precisely the same as, yet closely associated with, this kind of phenomenon are incidents of children who were isolated, confined, or restricted by malevolent adults so that their early social and sensory experience was severely limited and resulted in dramatic and often serious personality consequences. Similar limitations have been observed in children reared in institutional settings lacking the warmth of close human relationships, who subsequently may display some pathological personality features later in life, especially in the area of interpersonal relations (Bakwin, 1942; Freud and Burlingham, 1944; Goldfarb, 1943, 1944; Ripin, 1933; Stone, 1954).

The controversy (if it can be called this) about early infant isolation usually revolves around the old "nature-nurture" question, *i.e.,* "Does heredity or environment play the greater determining role in the development of the individual?" The data needed to answer the question (if it can be answered) are often obscured by the lack of uniformity in observation and reporting methods, a paucity of knowledge about the significant and relevant features of both the child's early environment and his hereditary endowment (especially with feral children), and the absence of valid and consistent evaluative techniques or instruments (*cf.* Stone, 1954). Nevertheless, the material accumulated over many years about feral, isolated, deprived, or restricted children may have provocative value in considering the effects of early isolation upon later growth and development; at least, directing our attention to unusual early experiences may serve to demonstrate the importance of some environmental influences superimposed over hereditary or genetic endowment.

Carl von Linne (Linnaeus) first introduced the name and concept of feral man in the 1758 edition of his *Systema Naturae.* While his accounts were based on poorly documented material from historical sources (which has always been one of the chief obstacles in this area), he was nevertheless credited with attempting the first systematic description of the wild child syndrome. In addition to Linnaeus' original nine cases,* Zingg's (1940) review lists in tabular de-

* For the reader's interest, these were:
   (1) The Lithuanian Bear-boy, 1661
   (2) The Hessian Wolf-boy, 1344
   (3) The Irish Sheep-boy, 1672
   (4) The Bamberger Cattle-boy, end of the 16th century
   (5) Wild Peter of Hannover, 1724
   (6) The Pyrenees boys, 1719
   (7) The girl of Cranenburg, 1717
   (8) The Songi girl of Champagne, 1731
   (9) Jean of Liege

tail thirty-one ostensibly well-reported cases together with histories and some details of their lives after returning to the society of human beings. The classic study of the wild boy of Aveyron by Itard (1932) has added impetus to the resurrected thesis concerning the importance of sensory stimulation and sense training at an early age for the normal development of human beings.

If in order to make some generalizations one were to group many cases of feral (or possibly severely neglected) children together, one could say, while still recognizing the limitations of the data, that the earlier these children were isolated from normal human society and the longer they stayed in this condition, the more difficult it was for them to give up their acquired "animal" characteristics and become humanized. In some cases, especially where mental deficiency was suspected, they made little or no progress whatsoever; in a few other cases, the children died soon after "capture" or lived only a few more years. Assuming that their intelligence was not defective, their chances of becoming "human" again were greater if the duration of their feral sojourn (or period of neglect) was brief, or if they were returned to society while still very young, usually between ages one through five, before they had passed through any critical periods of physical and psychological development, such as adolescence. If these children had had some appropriate human contact prior to being abandoned, especially within the first two years, their transition to normalcy seemed greatly facilitated.

Many of the children studied were reported to have been mentally deficient. They may have been so from birth, or may have become so owing to lack of sufficient social stimulation from human sources and the consequent failure to develop human standards of intellectual achievement and function. On the other hand, although the reported cases are not detailed enough to allow us to draw any conclusions about their personalities, we know that some children did not display intellectual impairment. They grew up to assume responsible adult roles and some few even excelled in the intellectual sphere. (Again, this seems particuarly true of those whose exposure was either brief or occurred after they had grown past the first five formative years during which the socialization into human society was well established.)

Of those children who were the victims of adult malevolence, one of the earliest and best documented cases was that of Kaspar Hauser (*cf.* E. E. Evans, 1892; von Feuerbach, 1833) who appeared on the streets of Nuremberg in 1828 at about age seventeen apparently after having been confined in a dungeon alone for most of those years. (It was suspected that he was the illegitimate son of royalty, and had been hidden from the public eye for reasons of political expediency). That malevolence was indeed a characteristic surrounding Kaspar Hauser is attested to by the strange circumstances attending not only his violent death at about twenty-two years of age, but by the mysterious demise, as well, of Paul J. Anselm (Ritter von Feuerbach), the scholar who cared for and tutored the boy, and who defended his claim to royalty. The remarkable aspect of the Kaspar Hauser affair was the fact that when he was found, he could barely walk or talk, appeared to be intellectually defective and apparently had very minimal human contact during his early period of confinement. While he never learned to walk well and displayed other physical disabilities as well, under the patronage of von Feuerbach, the boy developed into an intellectually superior individual, allegedly demonstrating great endowment in academic and philosophical matters and is said to have displayed mystical, ascetic tendencies. If the observations concerning the feral children are valid, then it would seem reasonable to suspect that Kaspar Hauser *was* exposed to some human relationship very early in life; it may have been such stimulation which insured against his irreversible deterioration during the years of his imprisonment. Whatever the truth of the matter was, however, the answers will probably never be known; his case is anecdotally presented here in an attempt to illustrate the often dramatic, multivariable consequences of early social and sensory limitation. It would be beyond the scope of this book to present all of the cases of extreme social isolation reported in the literature and in experience, but the ramifications of the situation shed some light on the dynamics of similarly isolated or restricted children (Davis, 1940, 1947; Dennis, 1938, 1941; Dennis and Dennis, 1951; Evans, 1941a, 1941b; Gesell, 1941; Goldfarb, 1943, 1944a, 1944b; Hill and Robinson, 1929; Hutton, 1940; Kellogg, 1934; Mandelbaum, 1943).

Stone (1954) appropriately points out that these concerns are hardly new, and that accounts of attempts to determine the effects of early isolation or restriction go far back in history. He mentions Herodotus' account of an experiment in raising two infants in silence several centuries B.C., as well as citing the thirteenth-century historian Salimbene, who wrote about an experiment allegedly conducted by the Emperor Frederick II:

> . . . he wanted to find out what kind of speech and what manner of speech children would have when they grew up if they spoke to no one beforehand. So he bade foster mothers and nurses to suckle the children, to bathe and wash them, but in no way to prattle with them or to speak to them, for he wanted to learn whether they would

speak the Hebrew language, which was the oldest, or Greek, or Latin, or Arabic, or perhaps the language of their parents, of whom they had been born. But he labored in vain because the children all died. For they could not live without the petting and joyful faces and loving words of their foster mothers. And so the songs are called "swaddling songs" which a woman sings while she is rocking the cradle, to put a child to sleep, and without them a child sleeps badly and has no rest.

(Salimbene, cited in Ross and McLaughlin, 1949)

Other Suggestive Evidence

A notable exception to the idea of transient effects of isolation is the claim of increased receptivity to the benefits of psychotherapy, as well as reports of improvement of depressed psychotic patients exposed to conditions approximating the reduced sensory situation of the McGill study (Azima and Cramer, 1956a, 1956b; Azima and Cramer-Azima, 1957; Harris, 1959), in the hope of bringing a new integration and heightened feelings of security like those reported by the solitary sailors, polar isolates, lifeboat survivors, and mystics. The patients were placed alone in a darkened room, wore translucent goggles (to prevent patterned vision), and had their arms in cardboard cylinders (to prevent sensations of touch). They lay motionless on a bed, no one spoke to them, and they were fed and toileted in silence. These isolation periods ranged from two to six days, depending on patients' individual responses.

In spite of the fact that these already disturbed people did not show the mental changes reported by others—perhaps because they were already functioning abnormally to begin with—it was concluded that such deprivation resulted in a state of disorganization, even precipitating psychotic reactions in some cases. However, some types of patients, especially those in depressive states, seemed to show marked improvement, increased motivation, socialization, and assertiveness. Some were actually discharged as improved or recovered after the isolation; of these, not a small number had been long-standing "back ward" patients.

The efficacy of the isolation procedure in this study, and its relationship to the improvement or facilitation of recovery from a psychotic state, may be questionable for the reason that no conclusive evidence was presented to show that any change observed was the direct consequence of the isolation itself—mere attention from the experimental personnel, for instance, could have accounted for these findings. Practical experience in the clinical setting, however, has frequently led to the use of restraint or isolation of certain types of patients with desired benefits, suggesting that such a procedure tends to reduce internal activity resulting in a state of relative calm and increased responsiveness to the ensuing stimulation of psychotherapy. It is interesting to speculate that some types of disturbed individuals may very well be approaching normality in their response to isolation, and thus become more tractable and receptive to measures which are known to be effective with people who are less disturbed. Until we know more about sensory and perceptual isolation, however, such a notion must remain within the realm of speculation only.

Mental aberrations similar to those reported by others in isolation or confinement have occurred in pilots of high-speed, high-altitude aircraft, and can also be expected of astronauts who will eventually travel to other planets (Ruff and Levy, 1959; Sells and Berry, 1961; Wheaton, 1959). As a matter of fact, experimental isolation in a sensory deprivation chamber, and in simulated space trips, was one of the procedures used to select our current crop of astronauts. Operating in a severely restricted environment with extremely monotonous tasks to perform and little more than the same instrument displays to see, pilots have reported feelings of isolation, unreality, and dreamlike states. Hallucinations have also been experienced, and suggestions have been made that the so-called "flying saucer" sightings by experienced flyers have been a form of such hallucination. There is evidence to indicate that these feelings, called by some (including the pilots themselves) the *break off* phenomenon, occur at times in approximately one third of all jet pilots (Clark and Graybiel, 1957). The term *break off* is quite descriptive; it has been experienced as a panicked, anxious, depressive feeling of loneliness at the realization that the earth and other people are so far away—that one is literally "broken off" from the world.

As already mentioned, similar reactions have been evident in prisoners in solitary confinement, with a range of effects including tense pacing, restlessness, tension, irritability, and assaultiveness. Some prisoners exhibit a regressed, dissociated, withdrawn, hypnoid, and reverie-like state, with transient *hypochondriasis* ("imaginary," attention-seeking complaints) also observed (Schein, 1962). Prisoners of war in North Korea not only showed increased suggestibility under the stresses of confinement, but also had an extremely high death rate (nearly four out of ten—higher than at any time in history) from basically nonphysical causes, attributable presumably to psychological isolation similar to that seen by Spitz in his hospitalism studies. The Medical Corps had no name for this affliction that caused these numerous deaths among eighteen- to twenty-five-year-olds; the prisoners insightfully called it "give-up-itis."

Repetitive tasks in man-machine systems, such as long-distance driving, flying, assembly line production, continuous monitoring duty at isolated stations—all produce hypnotic, trancelike states that can impair mental efficiency. The hallucinations of cataract patients and the "phantom limb" feelings of amputees who can still feel sensation from areas of the body which are no longer attached (Bartlett, 1951) are also problems of lack of stimulation, or at least of the variable, changing, dynamic stimulation necessary to maintain normal mental functioning. The external environment and its influence upon behavior is increasingly being recognized for its role in a wide variety of practical situations such as these.

Finally, we might consider sensory and perceptual isolation from a different viewpoint. There is the widely accepted concept, very frequently used in other kinds of situations, of *need* or *deficit*. Just as deprivation of nourishment to tissues of the body results in increased activity which functionally produces co-ordinated physical responses designed to place the organism in a more favorable position to acquire nourishment in order to survive, so deficiency of external sensory stimulation may also produce behavior designed to acquire such stimulation, in much the same way. Nutrient qualities of stimulation could be responsible, in large measure, for the apparent need for stimulation, or stimulus-seeking behavior manifested by people who hallucinate, report discomfort, or actively attempt to stimulate themselves. If "stimulus starvation" occurs in early experience during certain critical periods of development, the effects may be as profound as in early malnutrition. In other words, it appears quite possible that one can be "starved" for stimulation, as well as for food, and the responses associated with such a state seem, at least dynamically, similar to any other kind of starvation (*cf.* Franklin, Schiele, Brozek, and Keyes, 1948). Exploratory behavior or curiosity might be thought of as a kind of "snack" with novel stimuli for its substance, just as a fully food-satiated person might partake of an extra delicacy or two between meals. When food, or stimulation, has been irretrievably withdrawn, it then becomes a prerequisite for integrated, intelligent, adaptive behavior.

CHAPTER **6** ⋘

Sensory Deprivation
and Perceptual Isolation

The hypothesis that an organism requires not only
stimulation but a continually varied sensory input for
the maintenance of normal, intelligent, adaptive behavior (Heron, Bexton, and Hebb, 1953) has been
subjected to experimental scrutiny by many investigators since the publication and amplification of the
original isolation studies begun at Canada's McGill
University in 1953 (Bexton, 1953; Bexton, Heron,
and Scott, 1954; Doane, 1955; Doane, Mahatoo, Heron,
and Scott, 1959; Hebb, Heath, and Stuart, 1954;
Heron, Doane and Scott, 1956; Scott, 1954; Scott, Bexton, Heron, and Doane, 1959). The initial findings of
the studies, of which the most dramatic was the occurrence of hallucinations, appeared to have confirmed
D. O. Hebb's prediction that cognitive and perceptual
disorganization would result from exposure to a prolonged period of reduced stimulation and decreased
variation in the total sensory environment (Hebb,
1949). Subsequent reports by some of the same investigators have refined and elaborated upon these results
in an effort to clarify the nature of the observed phenomena and to identify important contributing variables (Hebb, 1958, 1961; Held, 1961; Heron, 1957,
1961). In the course of such exposition, and with the

consequent spread of interest in this novel technique for studying perceptual and cognitive function, some doubt has been generated about the seemingly inevitable deteriorative consequences (Brownfield, 1964). More recent evidence, especially in connection with the possible therapeutic application of isolation to disturbed individuals, has suggested, with some exception (Cleveland, Reitman, and Bentinck, 1963), a facilitative or enhancing effect (Adams, Carrera, Cooper, Gibby, and Tobey, 1960; Azima and Cramer, 1956; Azima and Cramer-Azima, 1957; Azima and Wittkower, 1956; Azima, Wittkower, and Latendresse, 1958; Azima, Vispo, and Azima, 1961; Cooper, Adams, and Gibby, 1962; Gibby, Adams, and Carrera, 1960; Harris, 1959; Jackson, Pollard, and Kansky, 1962; Rosenzweig, 1959; Ruff, Levy, and Thaler, 1957). As a matter of fact, an evaluation of the mass of literature on the topic produced thus far, while not impugning the contribution of the McGill studies or the validity of Hebb's theories, has logically led to the conclusion that whatever the requirements of the adult human organism for external and varied stimulation, reduction or monotonous patterning of stimulus input will not alone produce major disruptive psychological effects; such results are the product of a complex interaction of personality, anxiety, expectation, and situational structuring as well as amount and patterning of external sensory input (Arnhoff, Leon, and Brownfield, 1962; Brownfield, 1964a, 1964b; Stare, Brown, and Orne, 1959). The highlights of the McGill experiments, among others, will be reviewed in the following sections in order to attain an adequate perspective of the field of isolation effects. A brief description of the general literature seems appropriate, as a starting point, for our purposes.

Major Research Projects

In addition to the original studies of stimulus reduction and decreased sensory variability conducted
at *McGill,* there have been at least eight other major
projects dealing with the same topic or variations of
it. These were (1) at *Princeton,* under Vernon and his
associates (Vernon, 1959; Vernon and McGill, 1957;
Vernon and McGill, 1960, 1961, 1962, 1963; Vernon
and Hoffman, 1956; Vernon, Marton, and Peterson,
1961; Vernon, McGill, and Schiffman, 1958; Vernon,
McGill, Gulick, and Candland, 1959, 1961; Suedfeld,
1962, 1964; Grissom, Suedfeld, and Vernon, 1962); (2)
at *Manitoba,* under Zubek (Hull and Zubek, 1962;
Zubek, 1963a, 1963b; Zubek, Aftanas, Hasek, Sansom,
Schulderman, Wilgosh, and Winocur, 1962; Zubek,
Aftanas, Lovach, Wilgosh, and Winocur, 1963; Zubek,
Pyshkar, Sansom, and Gowing, 1961; Zubek, Sansom,
and Prysiaznuik, 1960; Zubek and Welch, 1963; Zubek
and Wilgosh, 1963); (3) at *Michigan,* under Jackson and Pollard (Jackson, 1960; Jackson and Kelly,
1962; Jackson and Pollard, 1962; Jackson, Pollard, and
Kansky, 1962; Pollard, Bakker, Uhr, and Feverfile,
1960; Pollard, Jackson, Uhr, and Feverfile, 1961; Pollard, Uhr, and Jackson, 1963); (4) at *Miami,* under
Arnhoff (Arnhoff, Leon, and Brownfield, 1962; Arnhoff and Leon, 1962, 1963; Leon, 1963); (5) at *Duke,*
under the principal investigation of Silverman and
Cohen (Cohen, Silverman, Bressler, and Shmavonian,
1958; Silverman, Cohen, Shmavonian, and Greenberg,
1961; Silverman, Cohen, Bressler, and Shmavonian,
1962); (6) at the *National Institute of Mental Health*
(NIMH), chiefly by Lilly and Shurley (Lilly, 1956;
Lilly and Shurley, 1958; Shurley, 1962a, 1962b; (7) a
series of studies by the *U.S. Army Leadership Human
Research Unit* (Presidio of Monterey, California)

under Myers (Myers, Forbes, Arbit and Hicks, 1957; Myers, Murphy, and Smith, 1961; Myers, Murphy, Smith, and Windle, 1962; Myers and Murphy, 1962; Murphy, Myers, and Smith, 1962); and (8) considerable experimentation was done by a *Harvard* group affiliated with Boston City Hospital (Davis, McCourt, and Solomon, 1959, 1960; Davis, McCourt, Courtney, and Solomon, 1961), later extended by Solomon, Leiderman, Mendelson, Kubzansky, Wexler, *et al.* (Kubzansky, 1961; Kubzansky and Leiderman, 1961; Kubzansky, Leiderman, Mendelson, Wexler, and Solomon, 1958; Leiderman, 1962; Leiderman, Mendelson, Wexler, Kubzansky, and Solomon, 1954; Mendelson, Kubzansky, Leiderman, Wexler, DuToit, and Solomon, 1960; Mendelson, Solomon, and Leiderman, 1958; Solomon, Kubzansky, Leiderman, Mendelson, Trumbull, and Wexler, 1961; Solomon, Leiderman, Mendelson, and Wexler, 1957; Solomon and Mendelson, 1962; Solomon, Wexler, Mendelson, and Leiderman, 1957).

Numerous studies arising from doctoral dissertation research have also made important contributions, though they were not conducted on the concerted, well-coordinated scale of those mentioned above (Baxter, 1959; Camberari, 1958; Goldberg, 1961; Goldberger and Holt, 1958, 1961; Holt and Goldberger, 1959, 1960, 1961; Keller, 1963; Ormiston, 1958, 1961; Pená, 1963; and others). More recently there have been projects reported by Zuckerman, formerly with *Adelphi College,* and now at the *Einstein Medical Center,* Philadelphia (Zuckerman, Albright, Marks, and Miller, 1962; Zuckerman and Cohen, 1964; Zuckerman, Levine, and Biase, 1964; Zuckerman and Cohen, 1964b). Military interest, particularly in connection with human adaptation to space flight, is also well represented (Brown, 1961; Cameron, Levy, Ban, and Rubenstein, 1961; Chiles, 1955; Clark and Graybiel, 1957; Cohen, 1958; Dempsey, Van Wart, Duddy, and Hockenberry, 1957; Eilbert, Glaser, and Hanes, 1957; Freedman, Gruenbaum, and Greenblatt, 1960; Freedman and Greenblatt, 1959; Goldberger and Holt, 1961b; Holt and Goldberger, 1959, 1960, 1961; Ormiston, 1961; Peters, Benjamin, Helvey, and Albright, 1963; Ruff, Levy, and Thaler, 1957, 1959; Steinkamp, Hawkins, Hauty, Burwell, and Ward, 1959; Weybrew and Parker, 1960; Wheaton, 1959). A research group at *Tohoku University*, Sendai, Japan, represents at least one major foreign research effort reported in the literature of sensory deprivation (Kitamura, 1963; Nagatsuka and Maruyama, 1963; Ohkubo, 1963; Sato and Oyama, 1963), though others are undoubtedly in progress and will soon be published.

Books

The implications and ramifications of what has come, somewhat inaccurately, to be known as *sensory deprivation* are embodied in at least six different books published since the McGill experiments were promulgated in the professional literature, attesting to the great popularity of the topic among behavioral scientists and the imaginative, creative research possibilities inherent in the experimental situation itself. Also, because it is a "new" field, it has opened many avenues of inquiry, promising to provide a kind of rapprochement between diverse fields and to explain hitherto inexplicable psychological events.

Sensory Deprivation: A Symposium (Solomon et al., 1961) is devoted to the phenomena first examined by the McGill studies, but extended by other researchers with specific applications to the fields of neurophysiology (Lindsley, 1961), aviation (Bennett,

1961), clinical pathology (Ruff, Levy, and Thaler, 1961), early experience (Heron, 1961), and so forth, but since this is primarily a collection of papers presented at the 1958 Harvard Symposium on Sensory Deprivation and not published until 1961, it was current only up to the earlier date. Three other volumes, while not wholly concerned with sensory deprivation *per se*, nevertheless review the area prominently in one or more chapters, and attempt to draw out reciprocal relationships between the experimental findings of isolation and the particular contextual problem to which each book may be addressed. For example, Biderman and Zimmer's *The Manipulation of Human Behavior* (Biderman and Zimmer, 1961) contains a review by Kubzansky (Kubzansky, 1961) about the effects of reduced environmental stimulation on human behavior, but written from the standpoint of explaining how human beings can be forcibly indoctrinated, coerced, manipulated, and made more susceptible to suggestion or interrogation as in brainwashing. Fiske and Maddi's *Functions of Varied Experience* (Fiske and Maddi, 1961) treats the topic, in Fiske's review chapter (Fiske, 1961), as illustrative of the importance of stimulation in maintaining the normal growth and function of the stimulus-dependent organism while emphasizing the environmental stimulus conditions themselves as determining the response. In like manner, Broadbent's *Perception and Communication* (1958) touches upon perceptual isolation as disruption of the dynamic interchange between organism and environment with consequent perceptual and cognitive distortion. The fifth book, L. J. West's *Hallucinations* (1962) is unique in that it is largely devoted to sensory deprivation phenomena in the context of exploring the dynamics of hallucinations and other hypnogogic experiences produced in controlled human isolation experiments (Collier, 1963). Vernon's *Inside the Black Room* (1963) is an aptly written account of the series of studies which he and his associates performed at Princeton University. Focused largely on how interest was developed in sensory deprivation and how one series of problems led to others, the solutions and the results make interesting reading.

These six books represent a major scientific attempt to put isolation of the senses into a comprehensible perspective without resorting to vague and broadly encompassing theoretical interpretations of the psychoanalytic genre, or to a particular psychological discipline such as learning theory, Gestalt, transactional functionalism, field theory, and so forth, though all of these have been variously invoked at one time or another (Cohen *et al.*, 1958; Cooper *et al.*, 1962; Flynn, 1962; Goldberg, 1961b; Goldberger, 1959; Goldberger and Holt, 1958b; Goldberger and Holt, 1961c; Goldfried, 1960; Hebb, 1961; Kubie, 1954; Leiderman *et al.*, 1954; Robertson, 1961; Rosenzweig, 1959; Shurley, 1960; Teuber, 1960; Vosburg, 1958; Wexler, Mendelson, Leiderman, and Solomon, 1958). In this respect the reported effects of being sensorily deprived and perceptually isolated have defied orthodox theoretical interpretation and have relied mainly upon analysis from an eclectic, modified behavioral and physiological position, being applied in whatever context seems best to suit the problematical questions under investigation.

Bibliographies and Reviews

A perusal of the three comprehensive bibliographies (Arnhoff and Leon, 1962; Pollard *et al.*, 1961; Rosenbaum, Dobie, and Cohen, 1959) compiled to date which are connected with sensory deprivation, isolation, and confinement, adequately demonstrates the breadth and scope of associated problems, as well as suggesting the "snowballing" effect of a research area begun only eleven years before. The compilation of references cuts across diverse fields and includes brainwashing, experimental psychopathology, sleep, psychopharmacology, physiology, vigilance, and therapy, among others. Reviews, exclusive of those contained in the above-mentioned books, have likewise grown in quantity and quality. Particularly interesting and informative are those by the Group for the Advancement of Psychiatry (GAP Symposium, 1956; Solomon et al., 1957; Vosburg, 1958; and Wheaton, 1959). A full appreciation of the complexities, nuances, and controversies, however, can only be derived from a comparison of the various reviews, which usually reflect authors' theoretical biases (Anonymous, 1959; Arbit, 1960; Freedman and Greenblatt, 1959; Gruenbaum et al., 1960; Leiderman, 1962; Levy, Ruff, and Thaler, 1959; Pollard et al., 1960; Pollard et al., 1963; Ruff et al., 1959; Wexler et al., 1958). At least one review-type article has appeared in the literature of the Soviet-bloc countries (Svorad, 1960), though experimental research behind the "iron curtain" has gone largely unpublicized until very recently.

Popular Treatment

Popular magazine articles have sometimes over-dramatized or distorted the evidence of research in experimental isolation, with the unfortunate result that the general public has reached unwarranted conclusions (Anonymous, 1959, 1960; Croft, 1954). One series of such articles goes to rather questionable extremes in purporting to show a relationship between sensory deprivation and extrasensory-perception phenomena, based upon some ludicrous and dubious historical speculations on the treatment of witches in the Middle Ages (wrapped and immobilized in a "Witch's Cradle" in order to achieve occult powers). Comparable is some seemingly sadistic "experimentation" by one individual upon a girl named "Justine," who apparently lacked sufficient intellectual and judgmental resources to resist allowing herself, among other things, to be suspended from the ceiling (in the manner of the Whirling Dervishes) or to have her hands tied to her ankles for long periods, with her head covered by a leather mask (The Baron, 1963, 1964).

Such articles, which suggest that people perform similar experimentation on themselves or on others for the purposes of having "cosmic" experiences or for achieving magical mental powers, constitute a serious hazard to the psychological welfare of marginally stable personalities; uncontrolled and ill-advised procedures by those lacking knowledge of the real phenomena cannot fail to create further misconception and perhaps even tragic consequences. There is at present no evidence to support the claim of occultists that mental power is enhanced in the way they claim —simply by undergoing sensory deprivation. Knowing this, the mature, intelligent person will regard such sensational claims with appropriate skepticism. Fortunately, not all popular accounts are so distorted, and it is to the credit of publications such as *Science Digest* that interesting, informative copy can be produced for the layman which does not always misinform or distort. Frisch's article on "Solitude: Who Can Take It and Who Can't" (1964) is a good example, though still much oversimplified.

At least one novel, *The Mind Benders*, by Jack Kennaway (1963), fictionalizes Lilly's (1956) water-immersion techniques and presents the sensory deprivation thus produced as something sinister and threatening to sanity, which, of course, has not been the case in reality. To portray experimental isolation methods as somehow endangering national security by making a person so suggestible and weak-willed that he becomes a traitor, as *The Mind Benders* implies, does a great disservice to a promising research field; instead of regarding the experimentation as an adventure in quest of knowledge, it makes it appear to be man's dabbling in the Black Arts. However, Kennaway does possess some keen insights into the subjective experiences of some kinds of personalities, and the novel does excite the imagination. It has been adapted for the motion pictures (*The Mind Benders* —American International); both the book and the movie may be worth-while endeavors, if we allow for distortion and exaggeration.

The McGill Studies

Since the original McGill University studies precipitated the whole question of sensory deprivation and opened a new track for research, theory, and speculation subsequently to be developed, it would seem valuable to review their details here. (Bexton *et al.*, 1954; Doane *et al.*, 1959; Heron *et al.*, 1953, 1956; Scott *et al.*, 1959).

Method: The subjects of the experiments were male college students who were paid twenty dollars a day to lie on a comfortable bed in a lighted, semi-soundproof cubicle, 8 x 4 x 6 feet, which had an observation window. They wore translucent goggles which admitted diffuse light but prevented patterned vision. Except when eating or toileting, they also wore cotton gloves and cardboard cylinders extending from below the elbows to beyond the fingertips, thus permitting joint movement but limiting tactual perception. A U-shaped foam rubber pillow, the walls of the cubicle, the masking noise of the thermostatically regulated air conditioner or fan, and the continuous hum from the amplifier to earphones in the pillow severely limited auditory perception. Communication between subject and experimenters was provided by a small intercom speaker system, but such interchange was kept at a minimum.

Subjects were asked to stay in the cubicle as long as they could (usually three to four days), and during this period were prevented, as far as possible, from finding out what time it was. An experimenter was always attending, day and night, and subjects were informed that if they needed anything they should call for it. They were fed and they went to the toilet on request, with these breaks in the continuity of deprivation averaging two to three hours a day. There were minor variations of method in studies describing different aspects of the same experimental situation.

General Effects: As was expected, in view of the evidence for the onset of sleep following monotonous and reduced stimulation in man and animals (Bakan, 1955; Baker, 1959; Broadbent, 1953; Davis, 1959; McGrath, Harabedian, and Buckner, 1959), subjects usually spent the earlier part of the experiment sleeping. Later they slept less, became bored, and seemed eager for stimulation; they sang to themselves, talked, tapped the cardboard cylinders together or used the cylinders to explore the interior of the cubicle. They became restless, displaying random movement and later described their experience as unpleasant. The boredom may have been partially due to deterioration in the capacity to think systematically and productively, but the general unpleasantness of the situation made it difficult to keep subjects more than two or three days, despite the fact that the pay for a twenty-four hour day was usually more than double what they could ordinarily earn. Some subjects terminated before testing was completed.

Unusual emotional lability was noted during the experimental session. The subjects seemed very pleased when they did well on tests but became quite upset if they experienced difficulty. They commented on test items more freely than when tested outside the cubicle; and while most reported an elated feeling during the initial phase of their cubicle stay, there was a marked increase in irritability noted toward the end of the experiment.

On emerging from the cubicle afterwards, when goggles, cylinders, and gloves were removed, the subjects seemed dazed. Also reported was some disturbance in visual perception, usually of one or two minutes' duration. The subjects had difficulty in focusing their eyes: objects appeared fuzzy and two-dimensional and colors seemed more saturated than normal. There were reported feelings of confusion, headaches, mild nausea, and fatigue; some of these symptoms lasted in some cases for twenty-four hours after the session.

Effects on Cognitive and Perceptual Functions: Qualitatively, the subjects reported that they were unable to concentrate on any topic for a long period of time while in the isolation cubicle. Some who tried to review their studies or solve self-initiated intellectual problems found great difficulty in doing so. Consequently, they lapsed into daydreaming, gave up efforts at organized thinking, and allowed their minds to wander. A few subjects experienced "blank periods," during which they were unable to think of anything at all.

In attempting to measure some of the effects on cognitive and perceptual processes, the McGill group gave various tests before, during, and after the period of isolation. In one study (Scott *et al.*, 1959), they even exposed subjects to a series of propaganda-type lecture records on psychical phenomena, measuring the direction of change in attitude toward spiritualism on a Bogardus-type scale. Table I (see pages 105-111) summarizes the quantitative results (as far as possible) of experimental and control groups with p-values (statistical probability of significance) based on final differences scores. P-values for tests one through five are for the second post-isolation period (not shown); the scores indicated are those obtained immediately after isolation. The twenty-eight measures given were gleaned from three separate research publications, each reporting different aspects of the same experimental situation (Bexton *et al.*, 1954; Doane *et al.*, 1959; Scott *et al.*, 1959).

It can be seen from the table that certain tested functions were impaired after the isolation, *i.e.*, number series completion, word-making, Kohs block test, digit symbol substitution, Thurstone-Gottschaldt figures, transcribing, Delta blocks, picture anomaly, Kohler-Wallach figural after-effect, size constancy, autokinetic effect, color adaptation, movement after-image, tactual form perception, specific two-point limens, and spatial orientation. Some subjects were not affected at all, but the total result could be interpreted as reflecting deteriorating cognitive or motivational changes.

Hallucinatory Activity

Most interesting of all the observed results was the occurrence of hallucinations reported by the subjects while in the experimental condition. At first there were several rather puzzling references to what one subject termed "having a dream while awake." Later, while one of the experimenters was serving as a subject himself he observed the phenomenon, and the extent and peculiarity of these experiences was realized.

The visual phenomena, said the experimenters, were actually quite similar to what has been described in mescal intoxication and the hypnogogic effects produced by a flickering light. There had also been rare cases of hallucinations in elderly persons without psychosis (Bartlett, 1951), which, like the McGill subjects, involved no special chemical or visual stimulation. Since the experimenters did not ask their first subjects specifically about these phenomena, they could not know the frequency of occurrence among them. Their last fourteen subjects, however, were asked to give an account of any "visual imagery" they observed, and the experimenters' initial report (Bexton, Heron, and Scott, 1954) was based on these accounts: "In general, where more 'formed' (*i.e.,* more complex) hallucinations occurred, they were usually preceded by simpler forms of the phenomenon." Levels of complexity were differentiated as follows: In the simplest form, the visual field, with eyes closed, changed from dark color to light color; next came dots of light, lines, or simple geometric patterns (entopic phenomena). All fourteen subjects experienced such imagery, reporting that it was new to them. Still more complex forms appeared which consisted of "wall paper patterns" (eleven subjects), and isolated figures or objects without background, *e.g.,* "a row of little yellow men with black caps on and their mouths open; a German helmet" (reported by seven subjects). At the highest level, there were integrated scenes, *e.g.,* "a procession of squirrels with sacks over their shoulders marching 'purposefully' across a snow field and out of the field of 'vision'; prehistoric animals walking about in a jungle." Three of the fourteen subjects "saw" such scenes, including dreamlike distortions, with figures described as being "like cartoons." A curious fact noted was that some of these hallucinations were reported as being tilted or inverted at an angle.

Subjects were usually surprised by these experiences, and then amused or interested, expectantly curious to see what would happen next. Later these visions were irritating and subjects complained that they interfered with sleeping. Some control could be exerted over content by "trying": one could see objects suggested by the experimenter, but not always as intended. For example, one subject, in trying to "get" a pen, first saw an inkblot, then a pencil, a green horse, and lastly a pen; trying to "get" a shoe, he first saw a ski boot, then a moccasin, and finally a shoe. The imagery usually disappeared while the subject was working on a test, but not always if he merely did physical exercises or talked to himself or to the experimenter.

Hallucinations involving other senses were also reported. People could be heard speaking in visual hallucinations, and one subject heard a music box. Kinesthetic and somesthetic sensations were experienced by four subjects. One described a "miniature rocket ship" shooting pellets at his arm, and another kept reaching out to grasp a doorknob he had "seen," but he felt an electric shock. Two subjects experienced physical sensations which were difficult to describe; they said they felt as if there were two bodies overlapped, lying side by side and occupying the same space within the cubicle.

Feelings of "otherness" and bodily "strangeness" were also reported: "my mind seemed to be a ball of cotton wool floating above my body," said one subject; another said that his head felt "detached from his body." The experimenters associated these experiences with similar phenomena reported in certain kinds of migraine. Charles Dodgson (*pseud.* Lewis Carroll), author of *Alice in Wonderland,* was a migraine sufferer, and it has been suggested that Alice's bodily distortions were actually descriptions of the author's own experiences.

In summary, the investigators concluded that both changes in test performance and hallucinatory activity, induced merely by limiting the variability of sensory input, provided direct evidence for a kind of dependence upon the environment that had not been previously recognized. The results suggested that experimental subjects generally did worse on some tests than did the control subjects, both during and after the isolation; and that they became more susceptible to propaganda when exposed to it during isolation, though in this case both groups showed a significant change in attitude. That some of these results might have been attributable to general disorganization of brain function which involved hallucinatory activity and disturbances in cognitive and perceptual processes, was also suggested by abnormal EEG (electroencephalograph) patterns which occurred under conditions of perceptual isolation (Heron *et al.,* 1956).

TABLE I

MEAN SCORES OF EXPERIMENTAL AND CONTROL GROUPS ON TESTS OF COGNITIVE AND PERCEPTUAL FUNCTIONS IN THE MCGILL UNIVERSITY STUDY BEFORE AND IMMEDIATELY AFTER ISOLATION PERIOD: P-VALUES ARE BASED ON FINAL DIFFERENCE SCORES OBTAINED FOR EXPERIMENTAL AND CONTROL GROUPS[1]

TEST	SCORE BASIS	EXPERIMENTAL		CONTROL		
		N Before After		N 1st Test 2nd Test		p
1. Multiplication of 2 and 3 digit nos.**	No. seconds to report, regardless of correctness.	18 150* 100*		27 135* 110*		NS
2. Arithmetic catch problems such as "how many times greater is twice 2½ than half 2½"**	No. seconds to report, regardless of correctness.	18 90* 60*		27 85* 45*		NS
3. Number series completion. **	No. seconds to report, regardless of correctness.	18 100* 70*		27 105* 60*		.05

(Continued)

MEAN SCORES ON TESTS OF COGNITIVE AND PERCEPTUAL FUNCTIONS IN THE MCGILL STUDIES OF "SENSORY DEPRIVATION" AND "PERCEPTUAL ISOLATION" (CONTINUED)

TEST	SCORE BASIS	EXPERIMENTAL			CONTROL			
		N	Before	After	N	1st Test	2nd Test	P
4. Word-making from letters of a given word.*	No. correct words.	18	9.9*	15.8*	27	9.9*	16.1*	.02
5. Anagrams—making a word from a group of jumbled letters.**	No. seconds to report.	18	130*	115*	27	155*	130*	.10
6. Kohs Block Test.	No. seconds to correct solution.	20	1088	931	25	1095	762	.01
7. Digit Symbol Substitution (Wechsler).	No. correct substitutions.	19	59.9	68.2	24	52.0	74.5	.01
8. Thurstone-Gottschaldt figures.	No. correct identifications.	12	5.5	5.4	18	5.2	8.1	.01

(Continued)

TEST	SCORE BASIS	EXPERIMENTAL			CONTROL			
		N	Before	After	N	1st Test	2nd Test	P
9. Transcribing a passage of unfamiliar technical material.	No. seconds.	18	594	640	25	634	639	.05
10. Delta Blocks.	No. correct.	12	9.4	13.2	19	11.4	19.9	.01
11. McGill Picture Anomaly Test.	No. errors.	15	8.0	5.9	23	4.0	4.9	.01
12. Mirror drawing.	No. seconds.	12	219	108	19	223	103	.10
13. Attitude questionnaire on psychical phenomena.	Total no. points on Bogardus-type scale as follows: (a) Attitude—168 pts. possible, (b) Interest—45 pts. possible, (c) Importance—20 pts.	24a	68.7	106.5	35	73.4	91.5	.02
		24b	23.5	31.0	35	26.9	29.6	.01
		24c	9.0	13.0	35	9.4	11.3	.01

(Continued)

MEAN SCORES ON TESTS OF COGNITIVE AND PERCEPTUAL FUNCTIONS IN THE MCGILL STUDIES OF "SENSORY DEPRIVATION" AND "PERCEPTUAL ISOLATION" (CONTINUED)

TEST	SCORE BASIS	EXPERIMENTAL		CONTROL		
		N	Before After	N	1st Test 2nd Test	P
14. Critical flicker frequency.[2]	Not reported.	17	No difference	13	....	NS
15. Kohler-Wallach figural after-effect (fig. 36)[2]	Described by Kohler and Wallach in *Proc. Am. Phil. Soc.*, 1944, 88, 269–357.	17	Increase	13	....	.02
16. Size constancy: picking far disc that looks same as near one.	Difference in diameter between test and comparison discs.	17	Increase	13	....	.02
17. Visual acuity.	No. correct identifications of a gap in one of three broken lines (42 trials).	17	Improved	13	....	.10

(Continued)

TEST	SCORE BASIS	EXPERIMENTAL N	Before	After	CONTROL N	1st Test	2nd Test	P
18. Brightness contrast.	Thurstone's method (*A factorial study of perception*, U. of Chicago Press, 1944)	17		No difference	13	....		NS
19. Autokinetic effect.	Level of illumination at pt. when S reports movement stops: 2 trials.	17		Increase	13	....		.001
20. Color adaptation.	No. degrees rotation of saturation-reducing yellow polaroid disc to match surrounding white.	17		Increase	13	....		.01
21. Shape constancy.	Difference between altitudes of variable test triangle and comparison.	17		Decrease	13	....		.10

(*Continued*)

MEAN SCORES ON TESTS OF COGNITIVE AND PERCEPTUAL FUNCTIONS IN THE MCGILL STUDIES OF "SENSORY DEPRIVATION" AND "PERCEPTUAL ISOLATION" (CONTINUED)

TEST	SCORE BASIS	EXPERIMENTAL			CONTROL			p
		N	Before	After	N	1st Test	2nd Test	
22. Brightness constancy.	Not reported.	17		No difference	13	....		NS
23. Necker-cube.	Not reported (possible no. of reversals per time unit).	17		No difference	13	....		NS
24. Movement after-image.	S's report of after movement, timed on three trials.	17		Increase in duration	13	....		.05
25. Tachistoscopic perception.	No. correct recognitions.	17		No effects obtained	13	....		NS
26. Tactual form perception.	No. errors in identification.	7	2.06	2.70	20	2.63	2.03	.02†
			(Continued)					

TEST	SCORE BASIS	EXPERIMENTAL			CONTROL			
		N	Before	After	N	1st Test	2nd Test	p
27. Two-point limens.	Values on a standard aesthesiometer:							
	a) finger	5	1.70	1.75	20	1.75	1.60	NS†
	b) forearm	4	29.6	24.0	20	23.4	23.7	.15†
	c) upper arm	4	29.1	23.8	20	32.8	32.4	.05†
	d) forehead	4	19.8	19.2	20	9.2	9.2	.02†
28. Spatial Orientation.	No. angular deviations from starting point.							
	a) walking	7	112.5	135.0	20	146.5	102.8	.001†
	b) paper and pencil	7	40.6	56.4	20	58.8	53.3	.05†

1 p-values for tests 1 through 5 are for second post-isolation period (not shown); the scores indicated were those obtained immediately after isolation.

* Estimated from graphical illustrations; no scores reported otherwise.

** Also given during isolation, after 24 and 48 hours, and 3 and 6 days afterward.

2 This data appears to be the result of a second separate study.

NS Reported as Not Significant, but no p-values given.

† Mann-Whitney U-Test.

TABLE II

MEAN SCORES OF EXPERIMENTAL AND CONTROL GROUPS ON TESTS OF COGNITIVE AND PERCEPTUAL FUNCTIONS IN THE TWO PRINCETON UNIVERSITY STUDIES BEFORE AND IMMEDIATELY AFTER ISOLATION PERIOD: P-VALUES ARE BASED ON FINAL DIFFERENCE SCORES OBTAINED FOR EXPERIMENTAL AND CONTROL GROUPS.

PRINCETON TEST	SCORE BASIS	EXPERIMENTAL			CONTROL			
		N	Before	After	N	1st Test	2nd Test	p
1. 12-item adjective lists, presented aurally; anticipation method, w/2 sec. interstimulus interval.**	No. trials to criterion of 1 errorless trial.	4	19*	17.5*	4	22*	26*	?
2. Suggestion.	Hull body-sway technique.	4	"Unsuccessful"		4	....		?

(Continued)

PRINCETON II †† TEST	SCORE BASIS	EXPERIMENTAL			CONTROL			P
		N	Before	After	N	1st Test	2nd Test	
3. 9 lists of 15 adjectives each; anticipation method; 5 sec. interval.	Mean differences only reported: Exp. gp-Control gp., as follows:							
	a) Trials to criterion:	9	Pre: 0.4		9	Post: -0.7		NS
	b) Errors to criterion:	9	Pre: -0.3		9	Post: 10.3		?
	c) Percent overt errors:	9	Pre: -3.85		9	Post: -2.67		?
	d) Fluctuation cycles:	9	Pre: -3.2		9	Post: 0.0		?
	e) Efficiency ratio:	9	Pre: 0.06		9	Post: -0.22		?

* Estimated from graphical illustrations; no score reported otherwise.
** Also given during isolation, after 24 and 48 hours, and 3 and 6 days afterward.
† Vernon and Hoffman, 1956. NS Not Significant.
†† Vernon and McGill, 1957. ? No p-value reported.

TABLE III / MEAN SCORES ON TESTS OF COGNITIVE AND PERCEPTUAL FUNCTIONS (LEARNING) FOR EXPERIMENTAL AND CONTROL GROUPS IN THE UNIVERSITY OF MIAMI STUDY * BEFORE AND IMMEDIATELY AFTER THE ISOLATION PERIOD: P-VALUES ARE BASED ON FINAL DIFFERENCE SCORES OBTAINED FOR EXPERIMENTAL AND CONTROL GROUPS.

TEST	SCORE BASIS	EXPERIMENTAL			CONTROL			P
		N	Before	After	N	1st Test	2nd Test	
1. Six lists of 15 adjectives each, presented aurally; anticipation method; 2-second interstimulus interval; 5-second intertrial.	Gp. Mean scores reported for Exp. gp.-Control gp., as follows:							
	a) Trials to criterion:	12	18.2	13.0†	12	20.1	14.4†	NS
	b) Errors to criterion:	12	139.0	85.9†	12	150.8	106.5†	NS
	c) Percent overt errors:	12	17.4	14.4†	12	14.4	12.6†	NS
	d) Fluctuation cycles:	12	19.6	13.3†	12	23.0	13.2†	NS
	e) Efficiency ratio:	12	0.14	0.15†	12	0.17	0.07†	NS

* Arnhoff, Leon and Brownfield, 1962.   † Score after 48 hours at end of isolation period.

CHAPTER 7 ⋘

The Work Since McGill

Learning Studies

Two subsequent studies on the effects of experimental isolation, both conducted at Princeton University (Vernon and McGill, 1957; Vernon and Hoffman, 1956), were concerned with learning in human beings as a measure of intellectual, cognitive, and perceptual efficiency; and the hypotheses in both of these studies were opposed to what might have been expected in view of the McGill work. It was predicted that "sensory deprivation," the misnomer applied to the original isolation procedure, would *facilitate* the learning process because of the absence of extraneous inhibiting stimuli interfering with the acquisition of newly learned material. The first Princeton study (Vernon and Hoffman, 1956), using a forty-eight-hour isolation period and four subjects, revealed a significantly better performance for the experimental group, a finding consistent with the facilitation hypothesis. But the second Princeton study (Vernon and McGill, 1957), utilizing a seventy-two-hour period and a larger N of 10, not only failed to confirm the findings of the first experiment at the end of the longer period but also failed to demonstrate a significantly better performance for the isolates after forty-eight hours. (See Table II, pages 112-113.)

A third and more recent study at the University of Miami (Arnhoff, Leon, and Brownfield, 1962), utilizing the same learning task as the two Princeton investigations but reproducing the sensory and perceptual conditions of the McGill studies, failed to find significant facilitation or decrement in the performance of an experimental group with an N of twelve. (See Table III, page 114.) Neither deterioration nor facilitation hypotheses were supported and the investigators concluded that whatever the requirements of the adult human organism for external and varied stimulation, reduction or patterning of input will not alone produce major disruptive psychological effects. Such results are the product of a complex interaction of personality, anxiety, expectation, situational structuring, and amount and patterning of external sensory input.

The phenomenon of facilitation by reduction of variable sensory input has thus been shown to be untenable under the conditions imposed by the experimental procedures, although some qualitative performance differences were still observed. In general, there was less "disagreement" with the McGill findings in the Miami and second Princeton studies (*i.e.*, no facilitation) than in the first Princeton study; but "agreement" does not quite describe the results either, because there was no deterioration, *i.e.*, no hallucinations and no performance decrement.

A possible explanation of the observed discrepancies does not appear to be so much a matter of depth or duration of sensory deprivation as was formerly thought; it may require rejecting the notion that learning is facilitated or caused to deteriorate simply by reducing varied sensory or perceptual stimulation. The first Princeton study did not attempt to copy the original McGill conditions, nor was the sec-

ond essentially the same as the first. Had the Princeton study attempted to reproduce the physical or
sensory conditions of McGill, the results of the first
learning study might have been more congruent with
those of the second, and both could have been interpreted as a refutation of either the simple deterioration hypothesis or the hypothesis of facilitation, as was
the case in the Miami study. This outcome is strongly
suggested by an examination of the experimental conditions of the two Princeton learning studies, as compared with those at McGill, where, as we have seen,
learning was not the primary process scrutinized. The
degree of sensory isolation was more severe in the
second Princeton experiment and it more closely approximated that of the McGill cubicle; the differences, however, may be crucial ones for understanding
the divergent results.

In the second Princeton study, the duration of time
equaled that of McGill's. The experimental cubicle
contained only a bed; but the first design used both a
bed and a chair. The subjects in the first study had
free access to both objects; therefore, the degree of
movement permitted was liberal when compared with
the second study and the McGill experiment where
subjects were restricted to lying on the bed only.

A basic, and perhaps critical, difference was that in
the two independent series of studies, one group of
subjects spent the major portion of their time in total
darkness while the others always had a moderate
amount of light-stimulation to the retina. In the second Princeton study, word lists were presented by tape
recorder in the cubicle antechamber while the subjects
sat blindfolded on the edge of the bed; previously,
they had been let out of their cubicle for meals, toileting, and testing in the antechamber by the light of a
fifteen-watt red bulb. By contrast, there was always

diffuse illumination from a shielded forty-watt white bulb in the McGill study, but transparent goggles prevented patterned vision.

The McGill cubicle was only sound-attenuated, whereas the Princeton cubicle was soundproofed. There was constant noise from the ventilating equipment in the McGill situation, but great pains were taken to produce a considerable sound-loss (80 decibels) in the Princeton study. Here again is a condition which differed in such a way as to lead to some speculation about the necessity of having just minimal stimulation to insure organized thinking.

Doane *et al.* (1959) provided some important clues for understanding the mechanism of the occurrence of hallucinations which may, for the purposes of the present discussion, be regarded as a crude indicator of the severity of disorganization of thought processes, as well as the efficacy of the isolation procedure. They had some subjects wear both opaque and translucent masks; two cubicle subjects wore the opaque masks until an hour before the end of the experimental period, when they were then fitted with the translucent mask worn by the others. Of the eleven subjects who wore the translucent mask continuously, eight developed hallucinations. When the two subjects, only one of whom had reported having weak hallucinations under the opaque condition, were given translucent masks, both had immediate and vividly strong hallucinations. Five subjects, who were among the most persistent hallucinators with translucent masks, were also put into complete darkness. They all reported an immediate increase in vividness of hallucinations; but within two hours there was a reported decrease, three having no more hallucinations and two having them greatly decreased. When they were re-exposed to diffuse light, all of them reported that hallucinatory activity returned to the original level of intensity. It was further reported that two of four ambulatory subjects, who were not confined to the cubicle but who did wear translucent masks, had hallucinations.

The McGill experimenters suggested not only that diffuse light was only one factor in the hallucinatory phenomena, but that a disturbance in function may be greatest in the area in which restriction occurs. There might also be some spread of effect to other senses; for example, auditory hallucinations may result from reduction of visual stimulation. In other words, there may be some interaction between sense modalities which depend upon external stimulation. If there is any validity in their observations, then under conditions of almost no stimulation there should be less disorganization—as gauged in this case by the occurrence and strength of hallucinations—than under conditions of invariant diffuse stimulation (Vernon and McGill, 1960, 1962; Vernon, Marton, and Peterson, 1961). Such an inference is not inconsistent with the outcome of the Princeton learning studies discussed here, since there was no reliably significant difference found between the groups in either situation at the conclusion of the experiment. Such was also the case in the Miami study, in the static conditions approximating the McGill procedure; no instances of hallucinations, delusions, or other unusual phenomena were reported.

The Need for Varied Stimulation

The results of the McGill studies and the two Princeton investigations raise some question about that part of the deterioration hypothesis which suggests only that some stimulation is necessary for the maintenance of normal, intelligent, adaptive behavior, since lack of stimulation in one case resulted in cognitive impairment and the reduction or disappearance of hallucinations, and in the other no significant differences between experimental and control subjects could be consistently demonstrated and no hallucinations were reported. In the sense that no stimulation elicits no response, the McGill hypothesis is correct; this is not intelligent, adaptive behavior—or more precisely, it is not behavior at all. But if no behavior is manifested, then no inferences of disorganization are warranted, since the organism becomes almost "inert" when nothing happens in the environment for a long enough period. It seems, rather, that a minimal, diffuse, monotonous stimulation is one of the primary requisites for disorganization of cognitive and perceptual function; lack of such stimulation in the most severe deprivation of input may produce nothing but a lack of reactivity, or a kind of psychological "suspended animation." The fact that monotony may be a necessary but not sufficient condition for disorganization was demonstrated by the Miami group.

What really seems to be necessary for the maintenance of integrated behavior is varied sensory input. When hallucinations reportedly occur, or at least when they are of maximum vividness, some actual input is always present from one or more sensory sources. Hallucinatory activity may only be an attempt by the particular individual to differentiate and to structure the input so that it has content and meaningfulness, even if the resulting organization is bizarre because of reliance on internal frames of reference in the absence of external ones (Boernstein, 1957; Cohen *et al.,* 1959; Davis *et al.,* 1960; Flynn, 1962; Freedman *et al.,* 1962; Mendelson *et al.,* 1958; Shurley, 1962; Solomon and Mendelson, 1962; Vernon *et al.,* 1958; Vosburg *et al.,* 1960; West, 1962).

Silverman, Cohen, Bressler, and Shmavonian (1962)

described a situation during a sensory isolation experiment of short duration in which the subject, a female psychology student, was in a totally dark cubicle. Inadvertently, the black paper covering the observation window was moved so that a crack of light became momentarily visible to the girl. She immediately reported that she had perceived what she thought was a Rorschach card and began elaborating an intricate delusionary system around this accidental, fleeting stimulus. It was pointed out that this normally negligible incident was sufficient to produce a complex organization of associations about a topic with which the subject was "ego involved." If one isolated stimulus against the background of monotony, or no stimulation, can evoke such complex behavior, then a continually varied sensory environment would undoubtedly seem necessary for the maintenance of such behavior. When variation is lacking, but a constant input is present, in spite of adaptation the organism "behaves" a little differently than if there is relatively no stimulation whatsoever; relatively little, if anything, happens.

Studies in which severe reduction of sensory input, especially kinesthetic, is achieved by actual immersion in water heated to body temperature (Lilly, 1956; Lilly and Shurley, 1958; Shurley, 1960, 1962; Walters *et al.,* 1962) have demonstrated that hallucinations and disorganization of thinking ensue with such rapidity that by the end of two or three hours the subject finds it difficult to continue (though females seem to tolerate these conditions better and longer than males). This is reminiscent of the increased activity reported by the McGill subjects who were placed in darkness after being in diffuse stimulation; the hallucinations began to disappear with the passage of a time period roughly equivalent to that of the water-tank experiments. In both cases, the rapid change from a condition of stimulation to one of relatively no stimulation resulted in increased hallucinatory activity, that is, disorganization of thinking. The change, in itself, may represent a variability of stimulation to which the organism responds with greater effort and energy by attempting to structure perception; when finally there is nothing to perceive, the situation becomes threatening. The process of *deafferentiation* may be so overwhelming that it represents a threat to one's very experience of existence, a state which, in the final analysis, may only be determined by the ability to respond to stimuli.

Other supporting evidence that change and variation are essential for organized functioning is the light-deprived subjects' responses upon being re-exposed to light (Doane *et al.*, 1959); hallucinatory activity immediately reappeared with the original vividness. Again, hallucinations may be a kind of homeostatic attempt to structure perception in the presence of stimulation which falls short of its mark because of the lack of anything to differentiate. Time distortions, too, have been reported, the subjects' tendency generally being to underestimate the duration of isolation (Lilly, 1956; Lilly and Shurley, 1958), an expected result if no progression of temporal events is perceived.

Defining Sensory Deprivation

Solomon, Leiderman, Mendelson, and Wexler (1957), in their review of the literature, feel that only three kinds of experimental conditions have been used or observed in sensory deprivation. The first is *reduced patterning of stimuli,* under which they classify the McGill procedure as a prime example. The second is the *reduction of absolute levels of stimuli,* like that which they feel Lilly accomplished by submerging himself nude, in water heated close to body temperature. The third type, according to Solomon *et al.*, is the *imposed structuring of stimuli*, by which they mean a narrowing down of the variety of sensory and perceptual experience to an invariant level. They cite observations of the mental functioning of normal subjects and polio patients in a tank-type respirator who, because of their inability to move or to see anything more than what is reflected in their mirrors, or to hear much more than the monotonous sound of the tank's bellows and motor, are, they feel, placed in a deprivation situation and respond with psychotic-like behavior (Mendelson and Foley, 1956; Mendelson *et al.*, 1958).

Other researchers have observed different cognitive and perceptual effects in sensory deprivation and perceptual isolation, but it becomes increasingly apparent that there is little consistency and stability with regard to the relationship between invariant stimulation and no stimulation whatsoever (Arnhoff *et al.*, 1962; Lilly, 1956; Myers and Murphy, 1962; Silverman *et al.*, 1962; Solomon and Mendelson, 1962; Zubek *et al.*, 1961; Zuckerman *et al.*, 1962; Zuckerman and Cohen, 1963). Because of lack of uniformity in results, questions are frequently raised about the contributing roles of variables, such as suggestion, motivation, personality, past experience, expectation, and situational structuring; the original problem and focus on stimulus conditions sometimes seem largely neglected. This is especially unfortunate since Hebb's theories (1949) concerning the need for continuous, variable, sensory stimulation in order to maintain normal, intelligent, adaptive behavior engendered the isolation studies in the first place. Kubzansky (1961) does, in fact, differentiate between "sensory deprivation" and "perceptual isolation": stimulation is absent or markedly reduced in the former, and invariant, boring, and monotonous in the latter. Certainly the above factors are important in understanding observed responses; measuring instruments also determine the limits of response, but the primary importance of stimulation itself is not negated. It seems, rather, that subsequent investigations in this area have changed the central and basic variable, the stimulus conditions, and attributed the varying results to extraneous factors so as to explain the differences.

It seems crucial here to re-emphasize the fact that the original McGill studies were primarily concerned with the motivational, cognitive, and perceptual changes resulting from monotonous and boring stimulation, and not with actual *deprivation* or reduction of stimulation. In this sense they were imposing a patterning of an extreme sort. No one to date has ever succeeded in depriving a human being entirely of visual, auditory, tactual, kinesthetic, and olfactory stimulation simultaneously (to mention only some of the variables which are capable of being externally controlled); all of the studies cited in the literature have only "monotonized" and reduced the intensity of stimuli or increased the uncertainty of stimulus situations, but have not eliminated them completely. External stimulation was always present in the McGill cubicle in the form of low illumination, constant noise from the ventilating system, and no effective precautions against gross movement. While normal levels of sensory, perceptual, and social stimulation were severely reduced, it does not seem appropriate to call this "deprivation," that is, no stimulation whatsoever. Neither does it appear to be a case of "reduced" patterning of stimuli, but more likely "increased" patterning, because of the highly static, repetitive nature of diffuse stimulation which provides input with rigid regularity, *i.e.,* no changes or variation—just "sameness."

What the water immersion experiments (by Lilly at NIMH) did accomplish appears to be a relatively greater degree of stimulus reduction and decreased variation, especially exteroceptively and proprioceptively, but not an absolute reduction or elimination, as implied. In the Iron Lung respirator experiments (Mendelson and Foley, 1956; Mendelson *et al.,* 1960), too, where subjects were confined to restricted mobility and visual field while exposed to the repetitive, rhythmic machine sounds, stimulation was not absent, but the variety and intensity were markedly reduced and made so monotonous that the situation was not unlike the McGill cubicle or Lilly's water tank; no actual deprivation seems to be involved, except in degree. In view of this, the tripartite classification of Solomon *et al.* seems somewhat superfluous.

All the methods thus far reported to produce sensory or perceptual isolation (or invariant stimulation in the "deprivation" sense) make it appear that only two basic procedures are available to researchers in this area, as Kubzansky suggested. The first consists primarily of *decreasing the variation* of stimulus input to a near-static level so that the effect is that of imposing a monotonized structure on the environmental stimulus complex; this is what has been done in most of the experimental studies reported. The second, and perhaps more difficult, method is to *deprive the subject of stimulation* in all sense modalities so that while neurophysiological receptor systems remain intact, they become non-operational because of lack of stimulation. Since no stimulation elicits no response, there is reason to suspect that these two procedures result in qualitatively different outcomes. Attempts to produce this kind of situation have been only partially successful, since only relative reduction of stimulus intensity has been achieved without the complicating side effects of drug anesthesia or amputation. Somewhat more success attends deprivation of visual and auditory input because of the ease with which light and sound stimulation may be experimentally diminished with appropriate conditions and equipment (Fiske and Maddi, 1961; Hebb, 1949; Silverman *et al.,* 1962; Vosburg, 1958).

The terminology of research in this area has been almost as confusing as the problem of definition. Many experimenters and writers have used preferential terms in order to designate the isolation procedure and to suggest theoretical differences in emphasis and intended meaning as well as in the effect on the organism. The following have been culled from the literature and are presented as being illustrative of the variety of expressions utilized to describe either sensory deprivation or perceptual isolation:

1. sensory deprivation
2. perceptual deprivation
3. social deprivation
4. stimulus deprivation
5. sensory isolation
6. perceptual isolation
7. social isolation
8. stimulus isolation
9. sensory limitation
10. social limitation
11. sensory reduction
12. stimulus reduction
13. environmental stimulus reduction (ESR)
14. decrease in sensory variability
15. restricted stimulation
16. controlled sensory input
17. reduced sensory stimulation

18. reduced sensory input
19. sensory alteration
20. "Ganzfeld"
21. homogeneous stimulation
22. solitude
23. confinement
24. isolation
25. invariant input

The list will undoubtedly be enlarged as research progresses and the body of literature grows; it is hoped that a parsimonious trend will emerge whereby agreement on terms will eventually be reached and confusion eliminated.

Individual Differences

That individual responses may differ according to personality differences has been amply demonstrated by the fact that some subjects in isolation show one kind of response—for example, hallucinations, disorganization, performance deficits—and others show an entirely different kind of response—for example, no hallucinations, little, if any, disorganization, and perhaps some facilitation of performance. Not all the McGill subjects reacted to decreased variation with discomfort or annoyance, nor did Cohen *et. al.* (1958) report similar uniform reactions with their subjects at Duke. Twenty-nine people began the McGill study, while only eighteen were sufficiently "comfortable" enough to finish; there must have been both personality and motivational differences between those who did and those who did not finish. Silverman and his associates (1962) reported that, in a pilot study, individuals prediagnosed as schizoid personalities were more content and even liked the situation better than normal subjects; body-oriented subjects were less disturbed than field-dependent ones, and sex-role differences were manifested in projective responses. These same investigators gave anecdotal evidence of specific ego-involved behavior; subjects projectively perceived common objects in their studies or employment in a single, accidental, fleeting exposure to a crack of light; for example, a medical student saw an X-ray. The works of Azima and Cramer *et al.* (1956, 1957, 1958, 1961), Bakan (1955), and Harris (1959) lend credence and some suggestion of validity to these observations in the sense that schizophrenics, the subjects with whom the experimenters worked, can be considered a specific class of personality syndrome in that they display similar types of responses to sensory isolation, as distinct from the normal subjects thus far used in other studies (though most of the latter have tended to use unclassified, unevaluated volunteers or "warm bodies" for subjects).

Interestingly enough, it has been reported that Soviet astronauts ("cosmonauts"), after being exposed to isolation and weightlessness as part of their preparatory training for space flight, are said to have enjoyed this condition so much that all of them confessed that they could think of no better way to spend a vacation. It may very well be that schizoid personalities, as reported by the Duke group and as borne out by the clinical studies mentioned above, might make the best space pilots; if being body-oriented and concrete-minded are the most suitable prerequisites for survival in space, then such seemingly atypical personalities might be better equipped to do so. Personality differences may account for differential motivation in volunteering for space flight projects, but it is conceivable that motivation can produce the particular personality which finds need-fulfillment in such ventures. These considerations have opened whole new directions for research, not only concerned with space travel *per se* but intimately related to the entire field of personality dynamics and motivation.

Research conducted at Duke University Medical Center was concerned with some rather specific neurophysiological reactions of human beings in low-sensory-input environments. The reports have yielded much valuable information about resting catecholamine and hormonal secretion rates, central nervous system activity, peripheral vascular activity, respiration, liminal discriminations, and other functions (Silverman *et al.*, 1961; *cf.* Murphy and Cleghorn, 1954). Using Witkin's Rod-and-Frame procedure and Machover's Draw-A-Person Test to discriminate two distinct groups, they have also demonstrated significantly different responses from subjects classified as "field-dependent" and "body-oriented" ("field-independent"); these differences appear to be related to characteristic modes of interacting with the external environment by reliance upon external cues for a frame of reference (Cohen *et al.*, 1958). It was suggested that individuals who relied on field cues react differently from body-oriented subjects in a situation in which field cues are minimized or lacking. Field-dependent subjects consistently displayed less ability in discriminating sensory cues, remained more centrally aroused, tended to move around more, appeared uncomfortable, struggled more with feelings and fantasies, or denied them, were more suspicious, projected internal percepts more frequently and, when interview responses were grouped to get a rough index of "ego function," showed a greater degree of disorganization.

There was also some suggestion that the individual differences reflected in body-field perceptual relationships may not only be related to responses in an environment that exaggerates these differences and leads to more arousal in one group, but the results may also reflect differences in neurohumoral (noradrenalin) and physiological variables which may be either a function of body-field differences or a parallel expression of some underlying central nervous system differences between the two groups (Cohen *et al.,* 1958). These same considerations may account for the differential responses observed in experiments with psychiatrically disturbed subjects.

Therapeutic Effects

As already noted, one of the more remarkable and seemingly contradictory suggestions developed in the course of research in sensory deprivation and perceptual isolation is that under certain conditions the isolation procedures may have positive beneficial effects for some persons. Actually, the results are not particularly surprising in view of the reported personality changes and reintegration experienced by solitary sailors, life-boat survivors, polar isolates, and others who have spent long periods of time alone in a monotonous, unchanging environment. Accounts of ego enhancement and reorientation of values have stimulated experiments designed to evaluate the efficacy of controlled environmental stimulus reduction in bringing about an amelioration of psychological disturbance.

Azima and Cramer *et al.* (in Montreal) were among the first to recognize the potentialities and to implement research in isolation with mentally disturbed individuals (1956, 1957; Azima and Wittkower *et al.,* 1956, 1958, 1961). In their experiments they exposed psychiatric patients representing four diagnostic categories to "partial sensory and perceptual isolation" for periods averaging about four days. Two basic sets of changes were observed: first, a "disorganization of psychic structure, which, according to the kind and quality of defenses, may lead to a psychotic state"; and second, such disorganization was usually followed by "reorganization of some aspects of a previously unsteady psychic state." The reorganization was reportedly accompanied by "constructive aggression" and an increase in motivation and socialization. Psychological testing suggested "no significant impairment in concentration and efficiency" and patients who, prior to the isolation, were refractory to more conventional psychotherapy, became more receptive and some actually improved to the point of being able to leave the hospital. In general, patients whose major pathological disposition was depressive seemed to benefit the most; while others, particularly neurotic and hysterical personalities, became more anxious and disturbed, displaying the discomfort and experiencing the phenomena reported by normal subjects. The implication, however, was that clinical perceptual isolation, or *anaclitic* therapy as the experimenters suggested (Azima *et al.*, 1958, 1961), could yield positive as well as negative therapeutic effects.

Investigating along the same lines, Harris (1959) put schizophrenic patients into sensory deprivation for shorter periods, finding that they tolerated the experience much better than normals and that in many patients the intensity of already present hallucinatory activity was reduced or eliminated. The Duke University studies (Cohen *et al.*, 1958; Silverman *et al.*, 1961, 1962) independently corroborated Harris' findings with respect to tolerance of isolation.

Additional researchers have pursued this line of investigation with nearly unanimous agreement as to the therapeutic value of partial sensory deprivation with psychiatric patients (Adams *et al.*, 1960; Cooper *et al.*, 1962; Gibby *et al.*, 1960; Jackson *et al.*, 1962;

Kubie, 1954; Leiderman *et al.*, 1954; Rosenzweig, 1959; Suraci, 1964). The one exception is a recent study by Cleveland *et al.* (1963), whose negative results and inconclusive findings were interpreted as suggesting little or no therapeutic value. In the light of the positive evidence, however, it would seem reasonable to conclude that some therapeutic advantage, particularly with depressed patients, is inherent in controlled experimental stimulus reduction. The relative paucity of studies and data tends also to temper any conclusions and we must withhold final judgment until further research has been accomplished.

Suggestion and Isolation Effects

In the attempt to explain differential responses by different subjects to sensory deprivation, and to account for the occurrence or nonoccurrence of hallucinations, many experimenters have explored the role of suggestion or prior verbal instructions (Camberari, 1958; Jackson, 1960; Jackson and Kelly, 1962; Jackson and Pollard, 1962; Kandel, Meyers, and Murphy, 1958; Leon, 1963; Levy, 1962; Orne, 1962; Schaefer and Bernick, 1962; Stare *et al.*, 1959). Their general findings seem to have established that the influence of suggestion via anticipation through prior knowledge, pre-established expectancy sets, and direct suggestion by the experimenter or the experimental conditions, plays a major role in producing the dramatic effects reported originally by the McGill group and subsequent investigations. There thus seems to be little doubt that suggestion is a factor to be contended with in interpreting the data of research.

Among the most important of recent experimental evidence, however, were studies by Rossi, Sturrock, and Solomon (1963) and Zuckerman and Cohen (1963). The former compared the effects of suggestion on imagery produced by hypnosis during sensory deprivation, and under conditions of drugs and placebo. Their results demonstrated rather convincingly that imagery (visual phenomena) was surprisingly immune to suggestion. The latter study tested the hypothesis that expectation or suggestion was responsible for the reports of visual sensations—using a control group and three additional groups incorporating increasing amounts of verbal and placebo suggestion. (A large sample of fifty-eight subjects was used.) The results suggested that prior knowledge and expectations were unrelated to reports of visual sensations while only the least structured and least meaningful type of reported visual sensations were found to increase with suggestion. In addition to this, while the role of direct suggestion in perceptual isolation has been largely over-estimated, the continuous reporting method (open communication channel between subject and experimenter) may be influential in producing reports of visual sensations, because such procedure "suggests" to the subject that the experimenter anticipates he will have something to report.

The effect of the sensory stimulus condition itself has again attained importance and focus in current research, and the role of suggestion has been somewhat minimized in accounting for the total response picture. Further support for the emphasis on the stimulus conditions and the physiological state of the organism, as opposed to the role of suggestion alone, is given by recent studies which have determined that movement restriction or physical immobilization plays a more important role in producing intellectual, cognitive, and perceptual changes (Courtney, Davis, and Solomon, 1961; Levy, 1944; Zubek *et al.*, 1963; Zubek and Wilgosh, 1963). Also, research with the drug Sernyl (1-phenylcyclohexyl piperidine monohydrochloride) has shown that sensory deprivation effects can be produced simply by modification or alteration of sensory and perceptual functions by direct selective action on sensory cortex, thalamus, and midbrain (Meyer, Greifenstein, and Devault, 1959). Administration of Sernyl results in demonstrable impairment of pain, touch, proprioception, and discriminative aspects of sensation. Motor function remains unimpaired until high doses are given, when ataxia and nystagmus occur. Subjects give reports of anxiety, depression, and fear, together with difficulty in thinking and concentration. In even higher dosage, illusional, delusional, and hallucinatory activity appear; there are also sensations of physical displacement similar to those initially reported by McGill subjects. Suggestion played no role in this study since the drug was being evaluated simply as an anesthetic for surgical procedures and the experimenters themselves did not expect the mental changes they observed.

8 ⋘

Other Variables in Sensory Deprivation Research

We have discussed some of the important considerations involved when a human being is deprived of varied stimulation, or stimulation *per se*. Among these were neurophysiological states, body-field orientation, absence or presence of diffuse stimulation, perseveration effects, early experience, suggestion, motivation, and personality. These considerations may be regarded as distinct factors capable of being manipulated experimentally or produced by the effects of such manipulation, and are thus treated as variables in research. Whether they are the independent, intervening, or dependent variables, as the traditional conceptualization would have it, would depend largely upon the focus of the research, the nature of the hypotheses, the experimental design, and the kinds of response measures used.

In order to understand the total response of subjects to the experimental stresses of perceptual isolation, it is suggested that all of the variables identified as possible influences on such a response be investigated systematically. For didactic purposes, and for the sake of convenience, these variables can be divided into three somewhat arbitrary groups: (1) subject variables; (2)

experimenter variables; and (3) situational variables. There are undoubtedly other important variables of at least equal significance which have escaped mention here and in the following outline; but in view of the relative complexity of data resulting from sensory deprivation research, it is to be hoped that this fault will be forgiven and implicitly recognized as partially dictated by lack of space, previously established criteria for schematizing the problem in this context, and the current author's ignorance.

I. SUBJECT VARIABLES. The importance of personality factors as possible determinants of characteristic reactions to decreased variation in the sensory environment, or to absence of stimulation, has already been suggested, not only here but by most investigators; however, few really clear-cut relationships have been established. The following categories include those subject variables which appear to require more adequate exploration and evaluation prior to exposure to isolation.

A. *Personality traits or character structure, i.e.,* the organization of patterns of psychological response which are more or less constant for an individual. These patterns would seemingly be quite relevant in partially determining the kinds of responses elicited in sensory deprivation. There have been a few isolated studies so far which have established both personality and related sex-role determinants manifesting themselves in differential responses (Arnhoff and Leon, 1963a, 1963b; Goldberg, 1961; Goldberger, 1959; Goldberger and Holt, 1961; Holt and Goldberger, 1959; Hull and Zubek, 1962; Ruff *et al.*, 1961; Walters *et al.*, 1962). Generally, these have established that certain kinds of personalities are able to tolerate deprivation better than others—females tolerate it better then males, though this finding is controversial—

and specific reaction patterns in deprivation studies are indicative of a subject's usual response to similar stresses when not in isolation.

B. *Level of personality integration* (ego strength). Holt and Goldberger (1959, 1960, 1961) describe how Rorschach measures of level of maturity of the ego appeared to correlate with various aspects of a subject's response in an isolation situation. It would appear vital to know more about how flexible and adaptable a human being is in an impoverished, remote environment, especially when practical problems of isolation have been, and will be encountered, probably, by space travelers. What degrees of psychological stress will they be able to tolerate when they are cut off from all the stabilizing cues of a familiar perceptual world? How will they react to the monotonous stimulus array of outer space? How much deprivation, frustration, and uncertainty can one experience before behavioral and emotional changes, concomitant with perceptual and cognitive changes, occur? Moreover, how realistic and appropriate will one's responses be; how well organized and how effective an expression of his intellectual capabilities?

C. *Socio-cultural factors.* Within this area are included such considerations as sex differences and the influence of cultural factors as they determine modes of response available to the subject. Pressure to participate in an experiment may be stronger for some groups than for others; this may inhibit or encourage certain responses, feelings, or behavior during the experiment, just as differential motivations may determine the reasons for a subject's volunteering (Bovard, 1959; Davis *et al.*, 1961; Hatch, Wilberg, Balazs, and Grice, 1963; Walters and Quinn, 1960; Vernon, 1963). This area has been largely unexplored to date.

D. *Psychophysiological state.* Ruff *et al.* (1957)

suggest that structuring the pre-experimental period has a definite effect on a subject's over-all response. At least some knowledge of recent life events and pre-isolation experimental instructions and information given to subjects can be extremely important determinants of the ultimate response: expectations, anticipations, and anxiety-producing information (or the lack thereof) could conceivably account for differences noted between subjects and between groups. However, the physiological state of the organism, as we have seen, plays an extremely important role in producing a response; and while research has revealed definite physiological correlates (Bexton, 1959; Cameron *et al.*, 1961; Cohen, 1958; Davis, 1959; Doane, 1955; Heron, 1961; Holt and Goldberger, 1961; Lindsley, 1961; Mendelson *et al.*, 1960; Meyer *et al.*, 1959; Murphy and Cleghorn, 1954; Riesen, 1961a, 1961b; Mendelson *et al.*, 1958; Silverman *et al.*, 1961; Teuber, 1961; Ziskind, Jones, Filante, and Goldberg, 1960; Zubek and Welch, 1963; Zubek and Wilgosh, 1963), there have been relatively few studies focusing on predispositional states or sets as determinants of the differential response (Peters *et al.*, 1963; Petrie, Collins, and Solomon, 1958; Petrie *et al.*, 1960; Vernon, 1959; Vernon and McGill, 1961).

E. *Motivation and attitude.* The most important and relevant aspects of the subject's dispositional states have been discussed in the preceding sections on motivation and personality. Obviously, as previously mentioned, the reasons behind volunteering to participate in an experiment may be related to differential responses. Differences in drive or motivation may also account for both facilitative and deteriorative effects, as well as for learning phenomena subsequent to isolation, when the organism appears to be searching out stimulation and increasing its activity level in the process (Bruner, 1959; Butler, 1957; Freedman and Held, 1960; Glanzer, 1958; Montgomery, 1954; Montgomery and Zimbardo, 1957; Meyers and Miller, 1954; Sipprelle, Long and Lucik, 1963; Smith and Lewty, 1959; Wendt, Lindsley, and Adey, 1963).

F. *Chronological age.* This aspect of sensory deprivation research has been notoriously neglected, or the limitations imposed upon investigators by the ages of the obtainable experimental groups have precluded any systematic approach to studying differential responses due to chronological age. Yet it is already quite apparent from work in early experience that differential responses can be reasonably expected as a function of age at the time of exposure to any experimental situation in which developmental stage is a factor (Bruner, 1959; Riesen, 1961). Human beings are continually changing or developing throughout the life span, and reduction of sensory and perceptual capacities, due to deterioration or maturation, is of primary concern to psychologists working at both ends of the developmental continuum, *i.e.,* child and developmental psychologists, as well as those interested in gerontology.

II. EXPERIMENTER VARIABLES. An important variable, unfortunately neglected too frequently, which is not measured or controlled, especially in the area under discussion, is that of the experimenter. In spite of his effect on the research design, his observations and interpretation of data, his biases and predispositions, the conclusions of research rarely take this into consideration (Kubie, 1954; Orne, 1962). Theoretical orientation, *a priori* assumptions about causal factors and responses, personal needs and strivings, and the inability of the experimenter to observe certain phenomena because of specific conflicts or defenses of his own, may all contribute to a restricted and possibly distorted evaluation of the interactions which occur. The use of statistical techniques, quantifiable methods, and carefully planned research may reduce the influence of the experimenter on the experiment, but can never eliminate it completely.

A. *Experimenter's expectations.* Just as the subject's expectations may in part be a function of the information received (Camberari, 1958) and influence his response, so too is the experimenter in part determining that response by his own expectations. By his structuring of the experiment in preparatory instructions, by his preconceived data-collecting methods, by his use of what he thinks are relevant response parameters, he contributes to variations in the subject's degree of uncertainty, repression, level of anxiety, and proneness to emotional arousal during sensory or perceptual reduction experiments.

B. *Experimenter's sex.* Sex, particularly that of the experimenter who places the subject in an isolation chamber, invariably leads to the arousal of feelings, attitudes, ideas, and fantasies which are related to the normal psychological interaction between sexes, but may become more pronounced under the peculiar experimental conditions of isolation. This area remains relatively unexplored to date, though subject's sex-determined responses have been studied.

C. *Experimenter's role in subject's life.* Depending upon the subject's perception of the experimenter as an authority figure, or of a particular stereotype, he may be guided in any expression of behavior that could affect his relationship with the perceived experimenter. This may lead to a suppression of response, or an effort to please, or any form of behavior designed to insure the continuance or abolition of the subject-experimenter dyad.

D. *Experimenter's "ignorance."* It is quite obvious that what an experimenter is unaware of may lead to his failure to consider important data. One of the more serious sources of error is the neglect of post-experimental interview situations in which the subject's reactions are being evaluated. The major source of information about subjective processes during the experiment is the introspective report. Failure to appreciate, for example, the subject's defensive maneuvers in response to the particular experimenter, or difficulty in reporting intrapsychic experiences because of the inability of the experimenter to elicit them, may lead to the omission of a significant body of information.

III. SITUATIONAL VARIABLES. The following factors have been suggested by many investigators as significant and relevant variables to be accounted for and independently manipulated before defining the stress-inducing elements in any isolation and sensory deprivation experiments (Zuckerman *et al.,* 1962).

A. *Deprivation or modification of sensory inputs.* What type of sensory input is altered? What is the quantitative extent of such alteration or deprivation of each separate sense modality, and what are the variations of combinations? The question has been raised frequently as to whether the deprivation of certain sensations, or combinations of them, is more disruptive to human functioning than other sensations or combinations (*cf.* Hochberg, Triebel, and Seaman, 1951).

B. *Restriction of tactility-mobility.* The limitation of the ability to move or to have physical contact with objects, and the means by which this limitation is produced, appears to be one significant variable deserving more attention. Is the subject's mobility restricted by the conditions of the experiment, or is it a function of self-induced enforcement at the experimenter's request? Perhaps the immobility is produced by the subject's fear; in this case, personality would enter into the picture. From what has been said previously about the importance of tactuo-kinesthetic sensations, it would appear that bodily perceptions are our anchors to reality and our sense of existence in the physical world; without these anchors it appears to be extremely difficult to maintain our orientation in space both real and psychological. The key to the mystery of schizophrenia, with its body-image distortions and perceptual disorganization, may well be in some impairment of proprioceptive, kinesthetic, or tactile mechanism. If drugs which produce physical anesthesia can have, as side effects, symptoms similar to psychotic distortions, then reduction of physical sensation, or some change in its characteristic qualities, may account for the dramatic corresponding behavioral changes observed (*cf.* Zubek *et al.,* 1963; Zubek and Wilgosh, 1963; Zubek, 1963).

Other relationships between these variables and their consequences have also been noted, and these deserve some attention here. Zuckerman and Cohen (1964), for example, observed that the chair method of confinement probably produced a maximum of kinesthetic feedback, and consequently few hallucinations or, as they prefer to call them, "reported visual sensations" (RVS). The bed method of confinement in a cubicle yields more RVS, while the tank-type respirator and water immersion techniques have never failed to produce some reports of visual sensations.

Position of body also seems to play a role in the reported effects: lying on one's back while in isolation appears to result in dreamlike sensations, while lying on one's side yields few or no reports of such phenomena. Oriented in a vertical position, the subject reports more vivid, well-integrated visual phenomena (Shurley, 1962).

C. *Social isolation.* The limitation of contact with other human beings and the loss of human and non-human cues in isolation can activate feelings of desertion or helplessness, in addition to other responses. It has been suggested (Hebb, 1949), as well as demonstrated innumerable times, that a sufficiently intense level of CNS activity develops under emotional stress to disrupt organized perceptual, cognitive, and behavioral functioning.

D. *Time uncertainty.* Uncertainty about the passage of time is associated with a failing orientation toward the external world. This could conceivably contribute to other factors in upsetting a person's usual habit patterns (Lilly, 1956; Lilly and Shurley, 1958; Vernon and McGill, 1963; *cf.* Vernon, 1963). Relatively little research has been done in connection with this problem.

E. *Periodic needs.* The imposition of requirements by the experimental situation to alter or modify eating, sleeping, smoking, toileting, and sexual habits, or the effects of the influence of these functions, is another important facet of research, and needs clarification.

F. *Escape.* Knowledge or ignorance about the ability to escape from the isolation conditions at will may have a profound effect upon subject response. When a subject is aware that he is being observed, or that he can terminate the experiment whenever he wishes, the response may be quite different from when there is no such escape alternative. Future astronauts and space pilots will probably experience profound psychological disturbance with the realization that all avenues of escape or return may be blocked (*cf.* Vernon, 1964).

G. *Continuity of isolation or deprivation.* The amount of activity required of a subject during an experiment may result in differential effects. The more a person in isolation is required to utilize his perceptual, integrative, and executive capacities, the more he is asked to organize his thinking, the more stimulation he receives as a result of these requirements in testing, the less likely it will be for disturbances of function to manifest themselves. One of the greatest faults of most sensory deprivation research is that too many things are asked of the subject—a situation which mitigates the very conditions which are the object of study. It would seem reasonable to expect, in the future, some definitive research relative to the amount of stimulation required to insure or negate sensory deprivation effects.

H. *Duration.* Different experimenters have utilized different time periods for isolation; this may in part account for divergent results. It is important to discover just how long a duration is required, under varying conditions, for deterioration or facilitation of function, or other phenomena, to develop. In this regard, ability to tolerate experimental sensory isolation, *i.e.,* duration of tolerance, may be related not only to personality variables but also to the nature of the stimulus conditions, the expectancies of the situation, the set, and the experimenter as well.

I. *Communication.* The presence of a signaling system between subject and experimenter has frequently been suggested as a relevant experimental variable. Regardless of the type of activity, it could be comforting to the subject to know that communication is possible; if he were not aware of such potentiality, his reactions to isolation could be more extreme. Being aware that one is being observed could also mitigate or preclude effective deprivation or isolation.

The purpose of identifying these variables is primarily heuristic; they may serve as a guide for future experimentation and as suggestions for research hypotheses. But the enumeration of these factors by no means implies that they constitute all of the relevant considerations for research. The only implication intended is that many variables deserve more attention than they have received in the past: that these variables are important.

Addenda to the Second Edition ««

Optimal Stimulation, Arousal, and Sensoristasis

Concepts of optimal stimulation level and arousal were first formally expressed in the mid-1950's, although there had been antecedent forerunners in the early 1930's, particularly in the formulation of the principles of homeostasis (of the vegetative functions) advanced by Walter B. Cannon in 1932. Also, in the early 1950's Stagner and Karowski published an introductory psychology text that utilized the notion of homeostasis in organizing and integrating the empirical data of behavior, but it was not until 1955, when both Donald O. Hebb and Clarence Leuba (Hebb, 1955; Leuba, 1955) made specific proposals about needs for variable sensory stimulation that psychology really began to grapple with experimental data and the issues they suggested. Berlyne (1960), Fiske and Maddi (1961), Burns and Kimura (1963), and, more recently, Schultz (1965), have attempted to develop theoretical alternatives to older conceptions of drive-reduction, conceptions that postulated that all primary motivation was directed toward reducing internal and external stimulation to a minimum. While these new formulations differ from each other in some important respects, they nevertheless share in common the recognition that prevailing drive-reduction theories of motivation and behavior are woefully inadequate in explaining and predicting complex behavior, both human and infrahuman, and that these are in need of revision or modification.

This impetus for a new conceptualization appeared on two fronts; one was the evidence of neurophysiological research relating to the role of stimulus input in motivation, and the other arose from parallel studies of sensory restriction, overstimulation, and vigilance. Only brief mention of some of the findings and speculations that have contributed evidence in support of optimal stimulation notions is made here, so we can go on to a consideration of some implications for motivation, with a few experiments bearing on the issue and a few suggestions for possible changes in current conceptualizations.

Arousal and the RAS

In the neurophysiological area, the work of French, Hernandez-Peon, and Livingston (1955); Duffy (1962); Lindsley (1961); and others resulted in the identification of the brain stem reticular formation (the dense neutral network forming a core extending from the medulla of the lower brain stem to the thalamus in the diencephalon) as that structure which plays a major role in alerting to attention and maintaining arousal. Fibers *descend* from this reticulum that influence the autonomic nervous system and body musculature, and *ascend* to projection areas on the cerebral cortex, so that this system, called the "Reticular Activating System" (RAS), contributes to and receives impulses from both directions.

The RAS itself thus has two major sources of stimulation: (1) sensory input from peripheral receptors and (2) cortical impulses (cf. Schultz, 1965). These stimuli result in diffuse activation or arousal within the neuronal network, and, in turn, send impulses to the autonomic system, the muscle, and the cortical projection areas. Stimuli from somatic, visual, auditory, olfactory, and visceral sources can act somewhat nonspecifically and interchangeably in activating the system; electrical stimulation of various areas of the cortex has also been found to lead to electrical activity in the RAS (French, Hernandez-Peon, and Livingston, 1955), which suggests that arousal can be initiated from either source and that the action is reciprocal. Thus Duffy (1962) infers that the interaction of cortical sources of stimulation with sensory sources in the RAS, in moderation, could lead to facilitation of arousal, but excessive interaction might lead to impairment or blocking of reticular activation in the cortex, resulting in disturbances of awareness and attention.

Lindsley (1961), noting the marked behavioral disturbances reported under conditions of both sensory deprivation and sensory overload, suggested that these effects can be explained in terms of the functioning of the "Ascending Reticular Activating System" (ARAS), which includes all fibers carrying afferent impulses thru the RAS. Since the RAS is strategically located so as to sample the incoming and outgoing impulses, the ARAS must be involved in alerting to attention, and it also serves an adaption function. Thus Lindsley sees the reticular formation as a kind of barometer, regulating or adjusting the relationship between input and output. He then assumes that the reticular formation has an adaptation level that becomes attuned to certain levels of activity. This level is, then, projected on the cortex, where it influences perception, learning, and emotion. The regulating system is disturbed or upset by disturbances in sensory input, *i.e.,* either sensory restriction or sensory overload.

Lindsley goes on to speak of an activation pattern discernible on the EEG, which is characterized by a reduction of the synchronized alpha rhythms and the induction of low-amplitude fast activity. This pattern is produced by sensory stimulation and has also been demonstrated by electrical stimulation of the reticular formation. Moruzzi and Magoun (1949) found that if an animal's brain showed an EEG characteristic of sleep (or low arousal) prior to stimulation, then electrical stimulation changed the pattern at once to one of arousal or activation. It was further found that a sensory stimulus from any sense modality had a similar capacity for arousal, behaviorally and electrocortically.

More recently, Weinberger and Lindsley (1964) demonstrated that stimulus offset or cessation can elicit electroencephalographic and behavioral arousal. They suggested it is the sudden change in stimulus conditions, rather than just the stimulus onset, or stimulation *per se,* which is responsible for cortical and behavioral arousal, and they concluded that *either* increase or decrease of stimulation can change the adaption level of the reticular formation.

Moreover, the RAS also gives evidence that it plays a role in the selectivity of attention. Hernandez-Peon, Scherrer, and Jouvet (1956) recorded responses from the cochlear nucleus in a cat during auditory stimulation with a clicker-cricket. During periods of relaxation, responses to the click were obtained by electrical recording from the nucleus, but when a mouse, fish odor, or shock was presented to the cat, the response to the click stopped. Direct electrical stimulation of the RAS *depresses* the response of the cochlear nucleus, and thus it was inferred that the RAS suppressed the response to the click during the presentation of the stimuli to which the cat was attending.

Thus it is apparent that both interoceptive and exteroceptive stimulation affect the arousal state that, in turn, determines the organism's capacity for efficient, adaptive, intergrated behavior. Hebb (1955) suggests that this arousal is really a general drive state that functions as a kind of "energizer," and is produced by the slower passage of sensory impulses through the ARAS, which terminate in diffuse stimulation over wide areas of the cortex. Impulses from the same stimulus source that travel faster provide more specific cortical stimulation, and function as a cue in controlling goal responses. Hebb goes on to support that intermediate levels of activation or arousal provide for efficient performance, but that low or very high levels are disruptive.

Thus an optimal level of cortical arousal (and, parenthetically, of reticular arousal) seems necessary for the establishment and maintenance of efficient, adaptive behavior. While both external and cortical stimulation are necessary, the absence of appropriate external stimulation can reduce the arousal capacity of the cortically produced stimulation. *What little stimulation is available is repetitive, and the ARAS becomes habituated to it.* (This is an important point because this habituation to repetitive stimulation is important in the consideration of the role of the level of external stimulation in effecting cortical arousal.)

The Role of Stimulus Variation on Cortical Arousal

Earlier, I referred to the formal expression of optimal stimulation concepts beginning in the mid-1950's, with some mention of the antecedents in the early 1930's, notably, W. B. Cannons's *Homeostatic* principles in *The Wisdom of the Body*

(1932). Actually, several other writers and researchers in addition to those I mentioned have considered the concept of a level of stimulation appropriate to the functioning organism. For example, "degree of energy mobilization" was considered by Cannon in 1929 ("Bodily changes in pain, hunger, fear and rage"); by Duffy in 1941, and again in 1951, degree of arousal was dealt with by Freeman in his book *The Energetics of Human Behavior* in 1948; level of arousal was one central issue in Hebb's *The Organization of Behavior* (1949) much as it was in Bindra's (1959) *Motivation: A Systematic Reinterpretation.* These all refer to a dimension representing the energy level or excitation level of the organism; an arousal or sensory continuum with deep sleep or anesthesia representing the lower end and epileptic seizures, and extreme anger, fear, or panic representing the upper end of extreme sensory stimulation.

Bindra (1959) reviews the automatic, somatic, and neural changes that take place within the organism under different levels of stimulation, and notes the existence of marked individual differences in both base level and degree of reactivity of these physiological functions. He describes three main points of difference between high and low arousal states. (1) The involuntary bodily processes function differently in the two states (*e.g.,* in high arousal, the sweat glands are more active and blood pressure and heart rate are elevated.) (2) Voluntary muscle activity is greater in high-arousal states. (3) The pattern of neural cell-firing is different in the two states, e.g., during sleep (low arousal) a preponderance of delta waves of high amplitude and slow frequency is characteristic of the EEG, while during excitement (high arousal) the pattern is characterized by rapid frequency and low amplitude.

Somewhere between the two extremes of arousal there must logically lie an area of optimal stimulation that results in efficient responding and learning, adapting, and integrating behaviors. All the theorists we have mentioned thus far have suggested this, although they differ in their conceptualizations of the role of the stimulus in the activation process, the dynamics of the arousal mechanism itself, and the response to variation and montony.

At too high an arousal level, the intense sensory bombardment may interfere with the delicate functions involved in cueing or guiding stimuli (Hebb, 1955), perhaps due to the "blocking" suggested by Duffy (1962). Thus, the intense stimulation may interfere with responses already in the organism's repertoire and may further prevent the acquisition of new stimuli. There are a wide variety of behaviors and performances which are thus handicapped by a high level of activation (Duffy 1962).

Cofer and Appley (1964) note that intense painful stimulation (which produces high arousal) can result in excited behavior and changes in skin conductance, muscle tension, blood pressure, EEG, and respiration. The person "wild with pain" is less capable than usual of dealing effectively with his environmental circumstances; thus, once the level of stimulation has exceeded the upper optimal range of stimulation for the individual, he is no longer capable of effective coping, and the result is something like "panic"—flight behavior, which is a disorganized, nonadaptive attempt to reduce the level of stimulation.

Stimulation levels falling *below* the optimal range are represented in studies of sensory deprivation and perceptual isolation where the effect of too little stimulation can be almost as disruptive as too much stimulation, although I question whether mere reduction of stimulation alone can produce these disruptive effects, or whether it is a reduction of stimulus-variability (Brownfield, 1964). Kubzansky *et. al* (1961) distinguishes between "sensory deprivation" as an absolute reduction of stimulus intensity and "perceptual isolation" as a reduction of stimulus variability without necessarily reducing intensity (though many studies compound both conditions, making it hard to distinguish between the two possibly different effects). I have reviewed a large number of studies that impose the two types of conditions differentiated by Kubzansky and have found that disruptive or disorganized behavior and performance were far less severe and less frequently reported in sensory deprivation (Brownfield, 1964a, 1964b, 1965), which suggests that lack of sensory stimulation has less effect on the arousal mechanisms of the RAS than does invariant stimulation (at least within the relatively circumscribed time-limits thus far used in most studies). For only one type of sensory restriction study, however, has there been uniform agreement about disruptive effects; these are the experiments in which tactuo-kinesthetic sensation has been absolutely reduced, as in water-immersion, physical immobilization, or under anesthesia with a drug that impairs interoceptive and proprioceptive sensation without impairing other sense modalities (cf. Brownfield, 1965). In these instances, the afferent stimuli from bodily sense receptors which continually send impulses through the RAS from different sources and at different rates (perhaps accounting in part for general arousal above a zero level) are markedly reduced or eliminated; such restriction, without deprivation of vision, audition, olfaction, or gustation has produced very similar disorganizing effects, and it may be that, while sensation is thus reduced absolutely, it is really the reduction of normal stimulus variability that accounts for the effects.

A subject in perceptual isolation is presented with a continuing series of similar stimulus events in which, in some experiments, his task is to detect stimulus change over relatively long periods of observation, as would be the case with the study of human vigilance behavior. Here the stimulation is of moderate intensity but repetitive and monotonous, offering little sensory variation. It has been suggested (Schultz, 1963, 1964b; Scott, 1957) that the decrease in efficiency found in vigilance studies is directly related to a reduction in sensory variability, and that performance reaches a higher level of efficiency under conditions that increase the variety and variability of stimuli, whether peripherally or task related, *e.g.,* such as when there is a higher signal rate, multiple stimulus sources, intrusive extraneous stimuli, etc.

"Most writers on the topic of restricted stimulation appear to accept the proposition that the normal and efficient functioning of the human organism depends upon external stimulation" (Fiske, 1961 p. 137). "They note that not only is the intensity of stimulation diminished but also that the minimal stimulation that does exist furnishes no information of value to the subject." (Schultz, 1965, p. 22). Because of the low level of arousal in the sensory deprivation of auditory, visual, and some tactuo-kinesthetic functions, Ss are not able to employ their own imagery to increase the level of stimulation, and thus, hallucinations, complex visual and auditory imagery, and severe cognitive disorganization is not generally reported (Brownfield, 1965). However, under conditions of monotonous invariant perceptual isolation, arousal level may be adapted to a higher level of stimulus input and Ss *are* able to utilize very slight changes (perhaps due to uncontrolled internal stimuli) for rather inefficient imagery that takes the form of hallucination. Cognitive disorganization, reported frequently under these circumstances, may be due to such inefficient, inadequate utilization of stimuli for arousal-level changes.

In 1964 (Brownfield, 1964a) questioned whether sensory deprivation or perceptual isolation always results in deterioration of organized behavior and cognitive functioning, since there were some suggestions in the research literature that some functions were either not affected at all or were even facilitated. Kitamura and his associates (Kitamura and Ohkubo, 1965) at Tohoku University, at Sendai, Japan, undertook to resolve the issue I raised, and in summarizing the results of a long-term, multifaceted series of studies, which they called "sensory deprivation" but which would be "perceptual isolation," according to Kubzansky's differentation, they concluded that the procedure "impaired higher mental functioning and facilitated lower mental functioning." By this they meant that lower-order functions, under control of the autonomic system, such as thresholds for gustation, vision, tactition, and audition, were lowered, while higher-order functions, such as Critical Flicker Frequency values, time estimation, and other functions requiring perceptual organization deteriorated. Activation (or arousal), as measured by EEG, was little affected once S had adapted to the monotonous stimulus conditions, except that Alpha, or supressed Alpha, waves were dominant for a greater part of the experimental period, suggesting general decrease of arousal level and consciousness. I would suggest that this result is due to the invariance of external stimuli rather than to absolute reduction alone.

In a personal communication, Kitamura (1966) granted

there may be basic differences between invariant stimulation and absolute reduction of stimulation, and he thus agreed with my suspicion that perceptual isolation impairs higher perceptual and cognitive functioning while enhancing functions dependent on the autonomic system; sensory deprivation would have the same facilitating effect on the lower-order processes but little or no effect on perception or cognition.

Thus, when the level of stimulus input falls below the optimal range of variability, gross distortions of overt behaviorial efficiency are observed. Such observations are borne out by EEG tracings taken of cortical activity under minimal stimulus input conditions, and there is a tendency toward a sleeplike pattern and slower frequencies in the Alpha range (Schultz, 1965, p. 22). While optimal stimulation level theories seem to deal with some "level" relative to arousal, the evidence suggests that it is not the level of stimulation *per se* which is so important for cortical arousal; but rather it is the level of sensory or stimulus *variation* that is important.

In support of this viewpoint, Davis, McCourt, and Solomon (1960) presented random visual stimulation to Ss confined in a tank-type respirator, and reported emotional disturbances, intellectual impairment, and hallucinatory phenomena similar to those resulting from constant light and noise. They suggested that the brain needs not simply changes in sensation but a *continuous "meaningful" contact with the outside world*. In their studies, montonous stimulation, when combined with random visual stimulation (which should have provided some variability), still resulted in cognitive disorganization; the experimenters offer "lack of meaning" as an explanation, but an alternative explanation could be that the random visual stimulation was below the optimum level required to alter arousal by overcoming the inertia of reticular adaptation; it created a kind of rhythmic "lockstep" which the visual stimulation could not break.

Freedman and Greenblatt (1959) used complete visual blackout and diffuse light conditions in their studies and also found the characteristic response differences I have mentioned above, interpreting the results in terms of absence of "meaning" rather than the specific nature of the stimulus field, although one might also suggest that "meaning" can be defined in terms of the intensity and variability of the stimulus field.

In summary, it might be suggested that under conditions of highly intense sensory stimulation (as in sensory overload) the intense sensory bombardment interferes with the delicate interaction involved in cue function. As a result, the so-called meaningfulness or patterning of the sensory input may no longer be perceived. Under conditions of vigilance or more extreme forms of sensory restriction, there is not enough varied stimulation to provide this "meaningful patterning." Thus a "sufficient" but not too high or too low level of sensory variation is necessary for the occurrence of optimal cortical arousal and adaptive behavior. Since "high variability" implies complete randomness and great frequency, and 'low variability" means complete patterning with no variation (or slow variation), it would appear that an optimal stimulus pattern is something in between, *i.e.,* "patterned randomness at moderate frequency," or some rhythmic pattern with moderately frequent changes. The intensity of stimulation, then, must exceed the lower threshold for arousal and must be variegated in pattern and/or time. If these conditions are not met, then arousal level is not sufficiently high enough to facilitate and maintain adaptive behavior.

Stimulus Properties Facilitating Arousal

I, and others, have brought into this discussion the idea that it is the meaningfulness of the patterning of sensory input that is crucial in influencing cortical arousal. There, inevitably always seems to arise a heated controversy about the meaning of "meaning." Granted that "meaningful" and "patterning" are vague terms on the surface, in recent years much effort has been expended in a more precise delineation of these stimulus properties capable of affecting arousal.

Berlyne (1960) proposes that stimuli have "collative" properties, which means that they depend on collation or comparison of characteristics belonging to different features of the environment. Collative properties include such characteristics as *novelty, complexity, indistinctness, incongruity,* and the like. To Berlyne, an advantage of collative properties, as he defines them, is that they can be discussed in the precise mathematical language of information theory. A "surprising" event, for example, would be one with high-information content. Jones (1964) suggests at least three statistical properties of stimuli: (1) information (the unpredictability or uncertainty of stimuli); (2) complexity (the objective randomness of stimuli series which are nevertheless predictable by subjects), and (3) fluctuation (the degree of alternation in stimulus series which are neither objectively random nor unpredictable.

However, Berlyne maintains that the concept of arousal has much in common with the older notion of "drive," so that the ultimate aim of the organism is to reduce stimulation to an optimum level, even if it has to increase stimulation first. Here is where Berlyne departs from other optimal-stimulation theorists, including myself. At issue here is Berlyne's proposition that no stimulation and stimulation *per se* both arouse or activate the organism, *i.e.,* under conditions of sensory restriction, and arousal levels rise until they become excessive thus the organism maneuvers to reduce arousal. Under excessive stimulation, arousal level also elevates, resulting in the same effect of producing drive-reduction.

My own argument against this is simply that the evidence from sensory deprivation and perceptual isolation research does not substantiate Berlyne's contentions for *cognitive* arousal. The Japanese have very clearly pointed out that lower-order functions are facilitated under conditions of decreased variation in the sensory environment, but that higher-order perceptual and cognitive functions (dependent on cortical arousal) under the same conditions are impaired. Studies in which absolute reduction of stimulation is achieved show only facilitation of or lowering of threshold for lower-order functions, but no impairment of cortical functions and/or the perceptuo-cognitive functions associated with it. Berlyne's arousal, then seems only appropriate for the vegetative processes and falls short in comprehensiveness when used to explain or predict the cognitive consequences observed.

Sources of Individual Differences

While space prohibits me from presenting adequately many
of the considerations supporting the view that stimulation
and not nonstimulation is the arousal source. I need only
mention briefly the numerous studies of the effects of differential stimulation in the early life of organisms on their adult
behavior. The data from studies by Beach and Jaynes (1954),
King (1954), Riesen (1961), Thompson and Schaefer (1961),
and others suggest that both decreased and increased levels of
early postnatal stimulation are capable of producing behaviorial differences in the later life or organisms. Restriction
of early environmental stimulation in animals has produced
drastic and enduring effects on emotionality, learning ability,
activity level, social behavior, and perception (Thompson and
Schaefer, 1961). Children reared in orphanages display lack
of attentiveness, impulsiveness, lowered cognitive capacity, and
lessened ability to relate to others (Goldfarb, 1955).

Increased early environmental stimulation in humans suggest more positive effects (increases in measured I.Q., for example) though the evidence is not conclusive. More reliable
data from animal studies indicate large gains in growth rate,
intelligence, ability to withstand stress (Thompson 1955,
1960; King, 1960; King, 1958), and even greater weight
and thickness of cortical tissue and an increase in total acetyl-
cholinesterase activity of the cortex (Bennett, Diamond,
Krech and Rosenzweig, 1964). Thus, a variety of response
systems may be affected by markedly different levels of early
stimulation and may in part account for individual differences
in optimal stimulation level in later life.

Generally, these studies support the contention of Riesen
(1960) and Thompson and Schaefer (1961), among many
others, that the growth and maintenence of neural structures
are dependent upon the adequacy of functional demands
placed on them by stimulation. Stimulation establishes the
function, and stimulation is needed to maintain the function.
The optimal level of sensory variation for each individual is
influenced by early postnatal levels of stimulation, and the
resulting level of cortical arousal is mediated through the

RAS and, more specifically, by the ARAS. Contact with a rich sensory environment would facilitate the development of differentiation of cue functions, of sensory modalities, and of events within modalities. An improvished early sensory environment would prevent such differentation and the fuller use of cue functions later in life. Because of the low activation produced, the organism would not perform well those learning tasks that require higher levels of activation. As Maddi and Fiske note: "Thus the restricted early environment may have a double-barreled effect; it limits or prevents the occurrence of crucial types of learning experiences, and it reduces the ability to learn from whatever experiences are available" (1961, p. 442). This does not imply that the activation level remains static throughout the remainder of the organism's life; the cumulative effect of sensory experience in the adult organism may possibly serve to modify the optimal range.

Genetic factors may also influence optimal arousal level, though here there is really little available evidence. Cooper and Zubek (1958) have studied the effects of an enriched and restricted environment on bright and dull strains of rats; differences between the two strains were eliminated by rearing the dulls in an enriched environment and the brights in a restricted environment. The dulls profited much more than the brights by enriched early stimulation, but an impoverished environment affected the brights much more than the dulls. Thompson and Schaefer (1961) were thus prompted to comment that "it seems quite clear that adding or reducing stimulation early in life will have differential effects to the genotype of the organism involved" (p. 97).

Sensory Variation as Reinforcement

After reviewing many of the experimental findings and considerations I have related here, Schultz (1965, p. 27) summarizes the major propositions of the optimal stimulation concept:

(1) Behavioral efficiency is a function of an appropriate level of cortical stimulation.

(2) This level of cortical arousal is highly dependent on

an optimal level of varied sensory input, *and we might add* (3) Arousal and optimal stimulation are meditated by the brain stem Reticular Activating system.

In order for "need" for stimulation as a motivational factor to be demonstrated, it must be shown that changes in sensory variation do, in fact, have reinforcing properties. If organisms exhibit evidence of learning in situations where the only apparent reinforcement is a change in stimulation, then the hypothesis of "need" for stimulation will receive some support. And the literature does provide much evidence suggesting that such behavior does occur in the absence of any reduction of the traditional homeostatic drives. I refer here to the numerous studies on exploration, alternation behavior, manipulation, curiosity, and play (and the studies that show a reinforcing effect of intracranial stimulation—the so-called pleasure centers-type studies of Olds and Milner) (*cf.* Berlyne, 1960; Bindra, 1959; Cofer and Appley, 1964; Dember, 1960; Fiske and Maddi, 1961; Schultz 1965) that do demonstrate the reinforcing effects of a change in stimulation.

Schultz reviews many experiments of this nature and concludes that it seems not unreasonable to postulate that a change in sensory variation can have reinforcing properties leading to the learning of instrumental behaviors. (Schultz, p. 28)

As Fiske and Maddi (1961) note: "When there is a large discrepancy between current level of activation and the optimal level or range for a given situation, the organism will typically engage in behavior designed to increase or decrease impact and thus to shift activation to reduce the discrepancy, thereby making effective instrumental responses more possible." (p. 15)

In drive-reductionist terms, "some behavior is tension-reducing while other behavior is tension-increasing." I might here add my own observation that it seems quite possible that most complex human behavior appears to be of the latter rather than the former type.

Sensoristasis: A Drive for Sensory Variation*

Sensoristasis is defined as a drive state of cortical arousal that impels the organism (in the waking state) to strive to maintain an optimum level of sensory variation. There is a drive to maintain a constant range of varied sensory input in order to maintain cortical arousal at an optimum level. Conceptually, this sensory variation-based formulation is akin to *homeostasis* in that the organism strives to maintain an internal balance, but it is a balance in stimulus variation to the cortex as mediated by the Ascending Reticular Activating System (ARAS). The word *sensoristasis* is used in the same sense in which Cannon (1932) spoke of homeostasis, and as such does not imply something set or immobile, but rather a condition that may vary, but that is only relatively constant. Thus, sensoristasis is concerned with a *fluctuating constant*—an optimal range that is capable of shifting as a function of task and subject variables. The control that serves to regulate the sensoristatic balance is the reticular formation which Lindsley suggests as serving as an adjuster of input-output relations. *The sensoristatic balance is disturbed or upset by conditions of sensory restriction and sensory overload.*

The essential corollaries of the sensoristatic model are seen as the following:

(1) The drive mechanism invoked in the concept of sensoristasis is synonymous with arousal as facilitated or mediated by the RAS.

(2) An optimal range or level of external stimulation exists that functions to influence the level of cortical arousal. The organism is able to function adaptively in his environment only when this optimal range is maintained. Too much or too little stimulation disrupts responses and prevents new learning.

(3) The organism will behave so as to maintain this optimal arousal level. Those behaviors that increase or decrease sensory variation to the optimal level will be reinforced, while those that increase stimulation above the optimal level will not be reinforced. Thus the organism is sometimes motivated to increase stimulation and sometimes to reduce it.

*Adapted from Schultz, D.P. *Sensory restriction: effects on behavior.* New York: Academic Press, 1965, pp. 30-32.

(4) The optimal range of sensory variation is capable of shifting as a function of several variables, such as task to be performed, present state of the organism, and level of preceding stimulation. More important, the range is subject to both inter- and intra-organism differences. Thus, one may speak of individual differences in need for sensory variation as well as differences over time within the same subject.

The following seven predictions are offered on the basis of the sensoristatic model:

(1) Conditions of reduced (or increased) sensory input will result in measurable changes in activation level.

(2) The sensoristatic drive state is induced by conditions of restricted sensory variation input and becomes increasingly intense as a function of time and amount of deprivation and or restriction.

(3) When conditions of sensory restriction (or overload) disturb the sensoristatic balance, the organism will exhibit gross disturbances of functioning, *e.g.,* perception, cognition, learning.

(4) When stimulus variation is restricted, central regulation of threshold sensitivities will function to lower sensory thresholds. Thus, the organism becomes increasingly sensitized to stimulation in an attempt to restore the balance.

(5) Organisms will exhibit evidence of learning in situations where the only apparent reinforcement is a change in sensory variation. Thus, under sensory restriction, increases in stimulus variability will have reinforcing properties, and under conditions of sensory overload, decreases in variability will have the same effects.

(6) There exist individual differences in the need for sensory variation. These individual differences may be partially due to early postnatal levels of stimulation that determine later adult patterns and optimal arousal levels.

(7) Reduction of the patterning of stimulus input will result in greater behavioral effects than simply reduction of the level of stimulation. Deprivation of variation in stimulation rather than level of stimulation *per se,* induces a more intense sensoristatic drive state. Hence, behavioral disturbances should be greater under perceptual deprivation conditions than under sensory deprivation contions.

References

BERLYNE, D. E. *Conflict, arousal, and curiosity.* New York: McGraw-Hill, 1960.

BENNETT, E. L., Diamond, M. C., Krech, D., Rosenzweig, M. R. Chemical and anatomical plasticity of brain. *Science,* 1964, *146,* 610-619.

BINDRA, D. *Motivation: a systematic reinterpretation.* New York: Ronald Press, 1959.

BROWNFIELD, C. A. Deterioration and facilitation hypotheses in sensory deprivation research. *Psychol. Bull.,* 1964, *61,* 304-313.

_____. Sensory deprivation: a comprehensive survey. *Psychologia,* 1964, *7,* 63-93.

BURNS, N. M., and Kimura, D. Isolation and sensory deprivation, in Burns, N. M., Chambers, R. M., and Hendler, E. (Eds.). *Unusual environments and human behavior.* London: Free Press of Glencoe, 1963, pp. 167-192.

CANNON, W. B. *Bodily changes in pain, hunger, fear, and rage.* New York: Appleton-Century, 1929.

_____. *The wisdom of the body.* New York: Norton, 1932.

COFER, C. N., and Appley, M. H. *Motivation: theory and research.* New York: Wiley, 1964:

DUFFY, E. *Activation and Behavior,* New York: Wiley, 1962.

_____. The concept of energy mobilization. *Psychol. Rev.,* *58,* 30-40.

_____. The conceptual categories of psychology: a suggestion for revision. *Psychol. Rev.,* 1941, *48,* 177-203.

FISKE, D. W., and Maddi, S. R. (Eds.). *Functions of varied experience.* Homewood, Ill.: Dorsey, 1961.

FREEDMAN, S. J., and Greenblatt, M. Studies in human isolation. WADC Tech. Rep. 59-226 (Contract No. AF 33 (616)-5663). WADC Aero-Medical Lab. Wright-Patterson AFB, Ohio, 1959.

FREEMAN, G. L. *The energetics of human behavior.* Ithaca, N.Y.: Cornell University Press, 1948.

FRENCH, J. D., Hernández-Peón, R., and Livingston, R. B. Projections from cortex to cephalic brain stem (reticular formation) in Monkey. *J. Neurophysiol,* 1955, *18,* 74-95.

HEBB, D. O. Drives and the C.N.S. (Conceptual Nervous System) *Psychol. Rev.,* 1955, *62,* 243-254.

HERNANDEZ-PEON, R., Scherrer, H., and Jouvet, M. Modification of electrical activity in cochlear nucleus during "attention" in unanaesthetized cats. *Science,* 1956, *123,* 331-332.

KITAMURA, S., and Ohkubo, Y. Studies on sensory deprivation, Part IV, *Tohoku Psychologia Folia,* 1965, *24,* 35-37.

LEUBA, C. Toward some integration of learning theories: the concept of optimal stimulation. *Psychol. Rep.,* 1955, *1,* 27-33.

LINDSLEY, D. B. Common factors in sensory deprivation, sensory distortion, and sensory overload. In P. Solomon, *et al.* (Eds.). *Sensory deprivation.* Cambridge: Harvard Univ. Press, 1961, pp. 174-194.

MORUZZI, G., and Magoun, H. W. Brain stem reticular formation and the activation of the EEG, *EEG Clin. Neurophysiol.,* 1949, *1,* 455-473.

SCOTT, T. H. Literature review of the intellectual effects of perceptual isolation. Defense Res. Bd., Dept. of National Defense, Canada, Report HR66, July, 1957.

SCHULTZ, D. P. Primacy-recency within a sensory variation framework. *Psychol. Rec.,* 1963, *13,* 129-139(a).

_____. *Sensory restriction.* New York: Academic Press, 1965.

_____. Spontaneous alternation behavior in humans: implications for psychological research. *Psychol. Bull.,* 1964, *62,* 394-400(b).

WEINBERGER, N., and Lindsley, D. Behavioral and EEG arousal to contrasting novel stimulation. *Science,* 1964, *144,* 1355-1357.

ZUBEK, J. P. *Sensory deprivation: fifteen years of research.* New York: Appleton-Century-Crofts, 1969.

Optimal Stimulation Levels of Normal and Disturbed Subjects in Sensory Deprivation*

A questionnaire, the Sensation-Seeking Scale (SSS), was administered to 70 normals and 70 randomly selected mental hospital patients. High scorers were classified as Sensation-Seeking and low scorers as Sensation-Avoiding. Sensation-Seeking was found more characteristic of normals, while Sensation-Avoiding typified mental patients as a group; females were less Sensation-Seeking than males; with increasing age all Ss tended to become more Sensation-Avoiding. A small group of patient and normal volunteers, representing extremes of scores on the SSS, were subsequently placed in sensory deprivation; differential responses seemed to relate to classification on the SSS rather than to diagnostic status. Sensation-Seeking Ss experienced discomfort, anxiety, boredom, and cognitive and perceptual disorganization (including hallucinations of a mild type), while Sensation-Avoiding Ss reported none, and also reported feeling better.

*Reprinted from *Psychologia: An International Journal of Psychology in the Orient,* Vol. IX, No. 1, March 1966. The research on which it was based was part of a larger project supported by Grant Number 63-7-8 (Y-51) from the State of California, Department of Mental Hygiene.

The author wishes to acknowledge his gratitude for the assistance of Miss Susan LeBlanc and Mr. Carl Fairfield in the administration of this research, and to Drs. Marvin Zuckerman and Raymond Wolfe for their constructive critical reading of this paper.

Zuckerman and his associates (Zuckerman, Kolin, Price & Zoob, 1964) have reported on their development of a "Sensation-Seeking Scale" (SSS) designed to quantify the construct: "optimal stimulation level." This construct was originally advanced by Hebb and Thompson (1954), Leuba (1955), Berlyne (1960), and Fiske and Maddi (1961) as an alternative to drive reduction theories which postulate that all primary motivation is directed at reducing internal and external stimulation to a minimum. Admittedly, concepts of drive reduction inherently recognize a kind of "optimal" stimulus-need level; under conditions of sensory overload, for example, behavior is seen as directed toward stimulus reduction. In sensory deprivation, however, *increasing* stimulation appears generally to be the organism's motivation. Zuckerman et al (1964) imply that differences between individuals as to what constitutes their "optimal" waking stimulation levels, particularly when such differences may be related to basic personality structure, are not adequately subsumed under usual notions of drive (tension) reduction. Whereas one may characteristically strive to increase stimulus input above level "X" in order to maintain normal arousal and functioning, another may actually require below level "X" to achieve the same ends.

Differences in tolerance for, and in response to, environmental stimulus reduction have been noted by numerous investigators as seemingly correlated with major personality variables (cf., Brownfield, 1964a; 1964b and 1965; Burns & Kimura, 1963; Goldberger & Holt, 1961; Kubzansky, 1961; Schultz, 1965, and Vernon, 1963). Of particular interest in this context are findings from studies of the behavior of mentally disturbed individuals during and after short-term or prolonged sensory deprivation (Adams, Carrera, Cooper, Gibby & Tobey, 1960; Azima & Cramer, 1956; 1957; Azima & Wittkower, 1956; Azima, Wittkower & Latendresse, 1958; Azima, Vispo & Azima, 1961; Cooper, Adams & Gibby, 1962; Gibby, Adams & Carrera, 1960, and Harris, 1959). These have demonstrated that some mental disturbances, especially those with depressive components, predispose one to manifest a paradoxically different response than normal persons subjected to the same conditions of reduced or monotonous sensory input. While normals apparently display cognitive-perceptive impairment, with delusions, hallucinations, greater awareness of their own primary thought processes, and consequent feelings of discomfort and anxiety, mental patients seem frequently to experience reduction or elimination of already active delusions and hallucinations, subsequent development of more adequate and "normal" secondary processes and, where depression is clearly identifiable, reduction of anxiety associated with reported feelings of comfort.

Within groups of both normal and disturbed Ss, individual differences are also noted; all Ss show varying degrees of tolerance for anxiety, discomfort and tedium. Thus there seems to be some general factor operating in both groups which characterizes one more than the other and which accounts for the observed differences within and between the two; it is hypothesized that this factor is the "optimal stimulation requirement." Revisions of our conceptions of drive reduction in the light of these considerations may necessitate changing treatment approaches in the clinical setting.

The SSS was designed and developed primarily to measure and quantify differential needs for optimal stimulus input. It seems to tap a broad stimulus-seeking tendency rather than specific behavioral traits as does, for example, Howard's Stimulus-Seeking Maze tests (Howard, 1961), which sample only alternation behavior, and have a non-significant correlation with the SSS (Zuckerman, et al, 1964). An inverse correlation between the SSS and anxiety as measured by the Multiple Affect Adjective Check List (cf., Zuckerman, 1960) was found, as well as a significant positive correlation with field independence as measured by the Embedded Figures Test (EFT).

The dimensions of *field dependence* and *field independence* as determined by Witkin's Rod-And-Frame Test (Witkin, 1949) were early demonstrated by investigators at Duke University to correlate with major response differences to sensory deprivation (Cohen, Silverman, Bressler & Shmavonian, 1958);

field dependent Ss, who tended to be schizoid personalities, tolerated isolation better than field independent ones, displayed fewer symptoms of anxiety and discomfort, and showed less affective, cognitive and perceptual impairment on a variety of tests and interviews. The SSS also seems to measure these field dimensions, but more broadly and non-specifically than the Rod-And-Frame apparatus; while there seems to be a similiarity between field independence and sensation-seeking, the two constructs should be regarded separately until more study and research have clarified the nature of this relationship.

The research reported in this paper was an attempt to determine the differential effects of sensory deprivation on normal and mentally disturbed Ss in terms of the characteristic stimulus requirements of each group. The construct of "optimal stimulus level" was utilized, and the SSS was employed to identify high, middle, and low sensation (stimulation) seekers before exposure to experimental isolation. The emphasis in this paper will be upon the relationships uncovered by the SSS between and among the two groups to which the questionnaire was administered. Comments and observations about the actual responses of a few of the high, middle, and low scorers in the isolation experiments will only be suggestive or illustrative of typical patterns emerging for each.

METHOD

Subjects

The SSS was administered to 140 Ss, half of whom were chronic and acute mental patients drawn randomly from the population of Mendocino State Hospital, and the remaining half were "normal" (i.e., unhospitalized, apparently normally functioning) Ss from the hospital staff, visiting summer college students, student nurses, and members of the faculty and graduate student body of the School of Education at the University of California, Berkley. There were 57 females and 83 males in the total sample; 26 normal females, 31 female patients, 44 normal males, and 39 male patients. Mean age for patients was 39.38 years, with a range of 15 to 64 years;

mean for the normal group was 36.55 years, with a range of 18 to 69 years. The mean difference of 2.83 years was not significant.

Table 1 shows the distribution of general diagnoses among Ss in the patient group.

Table 1.   Diagnostic Classification of Subjects in Patient Group[1]

Diagnosis	N
Schizophrenic Reactions	15
Other Psychotic States	2
Psychoneurotic Reactions	5
Sociopathic Personality Disorders	7
Personality Trait Disturbances	5
Alcoholism	26
Chronic & Acute Brain Syndromes	3
Transient Situational Reactions	1
Unknown or Undiagnosed	6

1. Classifications taken directly from patients' official hospital record.

This information was obtained from official hospital records *after* the SSS was administered and scored. Relative proportions in each diagnostic classification were fairly representative of the hospital population from which this sample was drawn, athough the alcoholic group is really somewhat underrepresented, since alcoholics constitute nearly 50 percent of the Mendocino State Hospital population.

In the final phase of the research reported here, Ss were asked to volunteer for experimental sensory deprivation; they were told simply that there was some evidence in the literature which suggested that the procedure might be beneficial to some types of mental patients, and that their participation might help clarify which types were helped and why. Some results of this part of the study are reported for 6 Ss, i.e., 4 normal volunteers and 2 patients. The Wechsler Adult Intelligence Scale (WAIS) was administered to all Ss who volunteered for the isolation experiment, and all were found to be of at least average or higher intellectual ability.

Procedure

The SSS was administered individually and in small groups over a period of about two months. The Scale was scored according to the criteria of Zuckerman, Kolin, Price and Zoob (1964); there are 34 pairs of statements on the questionnaire; one of each pair is considered a sensation-seeking statement, and the other suggests a preference for more conservative, withdrawing, and passive kinds of activities. The score was determined by the number of sensation-seeking statements with which the S indicated agreement by circling the letter of the preferred statement. Where it was difficult for S to decide which of the two sometimes unequal alternatives to choose, he was instructed to choose that with which he disagreed the least. The possible range of sensation-seeking scores was 0 to 34.

A critical range was established for the Scale on the basis of probability, and following the procedural suggestions of the research cited previously, scores of 24 and higher were classified as clearly Sensation-Seeking, while scores of 10 and below were regarded as definitely Sensation-Avoiding. This method enabled subsequent selection and identification of Ss from both patient and normal groups who represented extremes at each end of the score continuum; some of these Ss, as well as some from the middle range, were later exposed to periods of experimental sensory deprivation ranging from 6 to 24 hours in duration.

The scores on the SSS were analysed and compared between the two major groups and the various sub-groups within the sample. Means, variances, mean-errors, standard deviations and T-tests were computed to determine the significances of the differences found. Means for age groups were also computed to measure changes, if any, that might correlate with age; correlation coefficients were also calculated for both the patient and normal groups. and the results of this age-score grouping are very provocative. The number of clearly Sensation-Seeking and definitely Sensation-Avoiding individuals in each group was also counted to indicate if one orientation or the other predominated.

The isolation phase of this study took place in a light-proof, fan-ventilated, sound-attenuated room, approximately 9′ x 5′ x 10′ in dimension. All Ss wore earphone-type protectors of the kind used by rifle marksmen and jet aircraft mechanics to guard their eardrums from loud noise; these filtered out high frequency sounds, while the room itself took care of most low frequency sounds from external sources. Translucent goggles were also worn despite the fact that the room was absolutely dark; this was done to eliminate patterned vision when Ss were led through E's observation room to toilet on demand. The toilet, as well as E's room, was continually illuminated by daylight flourescent bulbs in order to reduce time cues to a minimum (e.g., day or night). Continuous intercom monitoring took place during the isolation run so that S could be heard talking, breathing, tossing, moving, eating, etc. All Ss were asked to lie quietly on a bed in the chamber and to report any thoughts, feelings, associations, etc., whenever they felt the need to do so. Tape recordings were made of all verbal communications during the isolation period, as well as during the post-isolation interview. The recorder was a voice-activated *Concord,* Model 330; this procedure allowed not only for later content analysis, but also for measurement of actual time S spent verbalizing. A supply of food jars and water was kept in the room within S's reach so he could feed himself without breaking the continuity of deprivation; the only breaks were for minor instrument adjustments and toileting, which averaged about one hour during each 24-hour period.

RESULTS

Group mean scores on the SSS for normals and patients, including major sub-groups, are shown in Table 2 along with related measures of central tendency. In addition to those groups indicated, there were four categories of patients with much too small an N to be included meaningfully in the table; these were the Psychoneurotics ($N=5$), the Sociopathic Personality Disorders ($N=7$), the Personality Trait Disturbances ($N=5$,) and the Unknown or Undiagnosed group ($N=6$), with means of 14.833, 18.200, 14.750 and 11.444 respectively. The range of scores for non-patients was 8 to 33, while the range for patients was 1 to 28. It is obvious that the variability was wide in both groups, which might be expected with so much heterogeneity, but it is also apparent that there are characteristic and consistent differences, despite heterogeneity between patients and non-patients, between males and females, and between the various other sub-groups compared, e.g., normals tended to be somewhat more Sensation-Seeking than patients; males in both groups tended to be more Sensation-Seeking than females of both groups, and the relative differences between patients and normals were maintained throughout the intercomparisons.

Table 2. Mean Scores, Variances, Standard Deviations, and Standard Errors of Means for Normal and Patient Groups on the Sensation-Seeking Scale.

Group	N	Mean	SD²	SD	SD_M
Total Patients	70	15.157	44.245	6.652	.8007
Total Normals	70	19.730	33.328	5.773	.6945
Alcoholics	26	15.923	30.690	5.540	1.108
Non-Alcoholic Patients	44	14.704	51.399	7.169	1.093
Schizophrenias	15	16.866	39.440	6.280	1.678
Female Patients	31	14.193	57.633	7.589	1.385
Male Patients	39	16.102	31.707	5.630	.9133
Normal Females	26	18.384	35.010	5.916	1.183
Normal Males	44	20.650	30.585	5.529	.8432

When the numbers of Sensation-Seeking Ss (i.e., higher scorers with 24 or above) were counted, 20 normals could be clearly identified as such while only 9 patients had equally high scores; Sensation-Avoiding Ss (i.e., lower scorers with 10 or below) were also found in both groups, but of these only 3 were in the normal group, while 19 were among the patients. Thus it would appear that high scores on Sensation-Seeking were more characteristic of the normals, while low scores typified the patients.

Table 3 shows the mean differences for the major groups and sub-groups compared in Table 2, together with indications of those which were statistically significant between the 5 and 8 percent levels of confidence (by T-test). As evident from Table 3, patients tended to be less Sensation-Seeking than non-patients, and female patients were somewhat less Sensation-Seeking than normal patients. The total non-patient group was more Sensation-Seeking than either non-alcoholic patients or female patients, while there were no significant differences between non-patients and alcoholics, male patients, normal females, schizophrenics and normal males. Most of the real differences occurred in comparisons of the normal male group with various patient sub-groups; normal males were significantly more Sensation-Seeking than non-alcoholic patients, alcoholics, female patients, and male patients. The other differences were not significant, though in almost every instance, except normals versus schizophrenics, normal subgroups tended to obtain higher mean scores than patient sub-groups, thus following a general pattern which seems to confirm the notion that mental patients, as a group, require less stimulation and thus seek it less in order to function optimally (at least according to their own notions of what is optimum for them).

Table 3. Mean Differences Between and Within Normal and Patient Groups and Major Sub-Groups on the Sensation-Seeking Scale; Significant *p*-Values are indicated and Levels of Confidence footnoted below.

Groups	Non-Patients	Alcoholics	Non-Alcoholics	Female Patients	Male Patients	Normal Females	Schizo-phrenics	Normal Males
Patients	−4.57***	−.76	−.45	−.96	− .94	−3.22	1.72	−5.49
Normals		3.80	5.02**	5.53**	2.62	1.34	−2.84	− .92
Alcoholics			1.21	1.73	− .17	−2.46	.96	−4.72**
Non-Alcoholic Patients				.51	−1.39	−3.68	2.18	−5.94***
Female Patients					−1.90	−4.19*	2.69	−6.45**
Male Patients						−2.28	.78	−4.54**
Normal Females							−1.49	−2.26
Schizophrenics								−3.76

  * Approaches significance
 ** *p*-Value is significant between the .05 and the .08 level (*t*-Test).
*** *p*-Value is significant at or beyond the .05 level (*t*-Test).

Another interesting relationship was found in comparing mean scores by age group for both patients and normals. Table 4 shows group means divided into ten-year age steps together with the *r* for each major group; a negative correlation be-

Table 4. Mean Scores of Patient and Normal Groups by Age on the Sensation-Seeking Scale together with Correlation Coefficients for Each.

	Patients			Normals	
Age Group	N	Mean	Age Group	N	Mean
15–25	13	18.92	15–25	17	22.14
26–35	13	16.69	26–35	10	21.00
36–45	18	14.00	36–45	30	19.23
46–55	19	14.00	46–55	9	17.11
56 +	7	11.42	56 +	4	17.50
r = −.33			*r* = −.25		

tween age and sensation-seeking is dramatically evident. As age increases, scores generally lower in both groups (r for patients was $-.33$, and for normals it was $-.25$), but normals scored significantly higher than patients at each age level.

The differences noted here suggest that optimal stimulation requirements vary between individuals and age groups in a generally predictable fashion; normals tend to be more Sensation-Seeking than the mentally disturbed Ss represented in this sample. An increasing tendency to avoid stimulation with increasing age characterizes both groups, but at different optimal levels so that the higher scoring group remains relatively better integrated than the lower scoring one in its functioning, i.e., it is "normal" and the other is not.

The experimental isolation phase of this study also suggested several interesting relationships between differential optimal stimulation requirements, as measured by scores on the SSS, and typical responses to restricted sensory input ranging from 6 to 24 hours. Of the 4 normals in this part of the study, two were clearly Sensation-Seeking, one was in the middle range, and one was definitely Sensation-Avoiding. The two patients were both female, and one was Sensation-Seeking while the other was Sensation-Avoiding. Two males and two females comprised the normal group.

All Ss who were clearly Sensation-Seeking on the questionnaire reported more discomfort, anxiety, and boredom than Ss who were definitely Sensation-Avoiding in orientation. As a matter of fact, Sensation-Avoiding Ss tolerated the experimental conditions quite well, subsequently reporting that they felt better, i.e., more comfortable, relaxed, calmer, less anxious, etc., than prior to isolation.* All normal Ss remained

---

*One highly Sensation-Avoiding female patient (SSS score=5), diagnosed as an anxiety neurotic with strong depressive features, found it so desirable in sensory deprivation that she pleaded to be allowed to remain in the room after termination of the period of study (6-hours), and it was only with much urging and great trepidation that she brought herself to come out. By contrast, another patient-S, a female who was clearly Sensation-Seeking (SSS score=28), diagnosed as paranoid schizophrenic with schizo-affective components, complained bitterly of the un-

in isolation until the end of the experimental period (which in all cases except one was 24-hours; one normal stayed for a prearranged 6-hour period), but during the post-isolation interview, high scorers said they would not wish to undergo the procedure again unless it would make a significant contribution to the treatment of patients; low scorers, however, made no such qualifications and seemed eager to re-volunteer at the earliest possible convenience.

When tape recordings of Ss' verbalizations in isolation were reviewed, quantitative differences were noted between high and low-scorers. Proportion of time spent verbalizing for any reason whatsoever was measured relative to total isolation time; it was found that high scoring, normally talkative, Sensation-Seeking Ss spent an average of about 13 percent of their time in some type of verbal communication, i.e., reporting, singing, talking to self, complaining, or making requests, while low scoring Sensation-Avoiding Ss, who were normally quiet, withdrawn, and not too verbal, used an average of nearly 30 percent for the same purposes. This difference was noticeable and consistent for all Ss in sensory deprivation.

Reports of hallucinatory activity also seemed to follow a specific pattern according to the dual classification scheme used here. High-scoring Ss frequently experienced reduced visual, auditory, and kinesthetic sensations, though there was nothing like the vivid, well-organized hallucinations earlier investigatiors have sometimes reported (cf., Brownfield, 1964b; 1965; Vernon, 1963; Zuckerman & Cohen, 1964). Sensations of bodily distortion or displacement, feelings as if the bed were rocking or tilting, reported subjective increases or decreases in room temperature, etc., were most common. A few Ss reported visual experiences ranging from flashes of light and colored geometric figures to "portraits of distinguished men floating in the dark at an inverted angle"; these were reported less, however, than the bodily sensations. Fewer still were the auditory experiences; 2 Ss reported hearing voices calling their names or saying indistinguishable phrases. By

---

comfortable conditions and gradually became so irritated and anxious that she terminated after 9 hours of an intended 24-hour run.

marked contrast, neither of the Sensation-Avoiding Ss described any strange or unusual experiences of any sort approaching those reported by the Sensation-Seeking Ss.

Fantasies and delusional ideas were very common among the high-scorers while none were evidently experienced by both low-scoring Ss and one high-scoring normal male. These fantasies and delusions appeared to be externalizations of primary thought processes, and seemed, to a large extent, to contribute to elevation in Ss' anxiety levels. Sexual preoccupation and fantasy was reported by 2 Ss, a male and a female; 2 more Ss, a normal male and a female patient, thought they were astronauts in a space capsule. Another, a normal female, was aware of the presence of someone else in the cubicle with her whom she described as "an old Negro maid." All Ss who fantasied also reported difficulty in distinguishing whether they were awake or asleep, and one normal female could not differentiate between her dreams while asleep and her fantasies while awake. The Sensation-Avoiding Ss reported only comfortable and relaxed feelings, slept soundly, and said they could think out their problems better in isolation without distraction from the environment.

DISCUSSION

In this study, Ss who obtained high and low scores on the Sensation-Seeking Scale reacted differentially, and predictably, to sensory deprivation as it was described here. High scorers manifested symptoms of cognitive and perceptual disorganization, such as the reported subjective visual, auditory, and tactuo-kinesthetic sensations, as well as delusions and fantasies. In addition, they reported feelings of discomfort, anxiety, and boredom; they also spoke significantly less than low-scorers while in isolation. On the other hand, Ss who were classified as Sensation-Avoiding (because of their low scores) showed none of the affective, cognitive, and perceptual symptoms experienced by the high scorers; on the contrary, they tolerated the experimental conditions well, and found the situation enjoyable, relaxing, comfortable, and anxiety-reducing. The fact that some Ss were disturbed mental patients and others were normals had relatively little bearing on individual response differences; the relevant variables appeared to be Sensation-Seeking or Sensation-Avoiding as determined by scores on the SSS, which in turn seems to reflect differential optimal stimulation requirements.

Administration of the questionnaire (SSS) to a large group of patients and normal Ss yielded both significant and non-significant differences, but all tending to lend strength to the suggestion that a randomly selected group of disturbed mental patients tends to be less sensation-seeking than a randomly selected group of normal non-patients. Sensation-Seeking, by simple frequency count, is more characteristic of normals, while Sensation-Avoiding is more typical of mental patients in general. Age and sex are clearly correlated with both classifications, and the relative differences between patients and normals is maintained throughout most of the comparisons of the various subgroups.

It appears that disturbed individuals, as well as the aging, are or become preoccupied with reducing stimulation and tension to an optimum level, while among normal individuals and younger persons, increasing stimulation to higher levels is characteristic. That the optimum level seems to decrease in mental disturbance, and with aging, is strongly suggested in this study. Allport (1953) regards such preoccupation with reducing stimulation as "clearly pathological," and even as early as 1939 Goldstein (1939, p. 197) felt that disturbed people were characterized as withdrawing, isolated, conservative, and stimulus-avoiding.

He writes:

In the state of isolation, as in sick people, the discharge of tension is in the foreground; the tendency to *remove* any rising tension prevails. In sound life, however, the result of the normal equalization process is the *formation* of a certain level of tension, that which makes possible further ordered activity.

He continues with:

The tendency to maintain the existent state is characteristic for sick people and is a sign of anomalous life, of decay of life. The tendency of normal life is toward activity and progress.

One might be tempted to accept Goldstein's formulations about the drive orientation of sick and healthy persons, especially in view of the evidence presented here and also by those investigations cited earlier which reported that mentally disturbed Ss reacted differently to sensory isolation than did normals. But Goldstein suggests that the tendency of the sick or mentally disturbed person is to *maintain* the existent state, i.e., to withdraw from active, stimulating life. While the facts seem to bear out this contention, the need still remains to explain why mental patients in sensory deprivation show not only better adaptation to these stimulus conditions (or lack of them), but reportedly improve or recover after being able to gratify and satiate the tendency to withdraw from stimulation. If we hypothesize that the Sensation-Avoiding person has a lower threshold for stimulation, and because of this he has become "super-sensitized" to normal stimulation levels, we can better understand why he responds paradoxically not only to sensory reduction but to (normal) sensory stimulation as well. If allowed to withdraw from "normal" environmental interactions on both the sensory and perceptual planes, the Sensation-Avoiding person seems to regain, perhaps through relief from sensory overstimulation, the ability to re-engage normally with the environment, as evidenced by reported improvement during and after isolation.

This notion involves the assumption that mental patients, among whom more Sensation-Avoiding Ss were found, are more receptive and responsive to environmental stimulation than are normals, and that a broadening of receptivity to a wider range of stimuli from the environment results in "overloading" and produces consequent maladaptive behavior and cognitive disorganization.

The findings of the present investigation seem to agree with others which have suggested that mentally disturbed Ss show the paradoxical response to sensory deprivation, i.e., they tolerate it better than normals, show little if any impairment of cognition or perception, and reportedly feel and behave better afterwards. If Sensation-Avoiding is characteristic of patients as a group, then the dynamics of the paradox become understandable; this study demonstrates the characteristic, and offers an explanation. The sensory conditions of the isolation experiment, besides possibly enhancing suggestive therapeutic effects, may provide patients with reduction of a kind of sensory overload in which the normal environment imposes too high a level of stimulation for Sensation-Avoiding Ss to be able to function as if they were normal and adaptive (i.e., Sensation-Seeking). When placed in a deprivation situation, they do show signs of an adaptive homeostatic process and appear to approach more normal modes of functioning.

Since Sensation-Seeking is more prevalent among the normal group, the implication here is that the normal environment does provide optimal stimulation, but deprivation of continuous, variable, normal sensory stimulation reduces the level below optimum, causing behavior and thinking to appear disorganized, impaired, and maladaptive. In this sense, hallucinatory activity, delusions, and fantasies appear to be attempts at raising the stimulation level by drawing upon the internal reservoir of primary processes in the absence of a supportive interaction wtih an environment in which secondary processes are the most appropriate and adaptive.

If, as suggested here, some mental patients are motivated to avoid stimulation and reduce tension by withdrawing from activity and engagement with the environment and those interactions that tend to raise the stimulus (tension) level, one might conclude that this is "pathological," and that therefore every effort must be made to force the patient in the opposite direction, i.e., toward activity and engagement. This conclusion, in fact, seems to dictate the philosophy of treatment in most mental hospitals; since it is felt that isolation and withdrawal is characteristic of pathology, then every effort must be made to avoid such a trend, and one must indiscriminately "push" patients toward behavior that characterizes the normal Sensation-Seeking person. Thus no distinction is made between optimal stimulation requirements of different individuals; everyone is expected to engage with the environment, to involve themselves in stimulating activity, to get out of bed in the morning and to stay out of the room and the ward, and ultimately to be active. This approach may actually retard some patients' recoveries, especially if they are in the sensation (stimulation) reducing or avoiding stage of a recuperative process. If the tension level in a normal, stimulating environment is too high for a patient because of his chronically lowered threshold for response, he might need the opportunity to withdraw and "disengage" in order to allow the natural homeostatic processes of adjustment to actualize. If he is thwarted and continually prevailed upon by the environment to respond to a wider range of stimuli, which he experiences more acutely than do normals, the opportunity for this adjustive homeostatic manuever may never occur, or at least be delayed until the slow process of adaptation makes normal environmental stimuli nothing more than background at a higher optimal level.

CONCLUSIONS

On the basis of the evidence in this study we may conclude that the construct: "optimal stimulation level" is an important and relevant variable in explaining differential reactions to varying levels of sensory stimulation, including those reported for normal Ss and mental patients in sensory deprivation. The Sensation-Seeking Scale appears to measure differential optimal stimulation requirements roughly but accurately enough, at least at extremes, to allow for predictions of the way Ss will respond to decreased variation and absolute reduction of the sensory environment. On the basis of score-classification on the SSS, one can expect high scorers (Sensation-Seeking Ss) to manifest cognitive, affective, and perceptual disorganization, to reduce their verbal output relative to normal levels, and to tolerate the conditions with negative affect. Low scorers (Sensation-Avoiding Ss) will not generally manifest the disorganization reported by the high scorers, will increase their verbal output, and will tolerate the conditions well, even to the extent of liking them and feeling therapeutic value for themselves in isolation.

The results of the administration of the SSS to a large group of Ss, both normal and disturbed, suggests that differences in characteristic optimal stimulation levels do exist despite heterogeneity of the sample, and that these differences determine the characteristics of the groups and of the response of those groups to sensory manipulation. In almost every comparison, non-patient sub-groups tended to be more sensation-seeking than patient sub-groups, though only some of the differences were statistically significant. Men were Sensation-Seeking relative to women, and this difference was maintained throughout the intercomparisons of the various normal and patient sub-groups sampled. With increasing age, Sensation-Avoiding tends to increase in both patient and normal groups (i.e., they are negatively correlated), but at every age level normals were relatively more Sensation-Seeking than patients.

In view of these findings, it would appear that our approach to the clinical treatment of mentally disturbed individuals, including milieu therapy, ought to be predicated on a recognition of individual optimal stimulation requirements, and procedures should be adjusted to insure that those requirements can be met. The opportunity should be afforded by differential treatment methods that allow for natural homeostatic adjustment processes to actualize in both high and low sensation-seekers.

References

ADAMS, H. B., Carrera, R. N., Cooper, G. D., and Gibby, R. G. Personality and intellectual changes in psychiatric patients following brief partial sensory deprivation. *Amer. Psychol.*, 1960, *15*, 448 (Abstract).

ALLPORT, G. W. The ego in contemporary society. *Psychol. Rev.*, 1943, *50*, 451-478.

ALLPORT, G. W. The trend in motivational theory. *Amer. J. Orthopsychiat.*, 1953, *23*, 107-119.

ARNHOFF, F. N., and Leon, H. V. Personality factors related to success and failure in sensory deprivation subjects. *Percept. mot. Skills*, 1963, *16*, 46.

AZIMA, H., and Cramer, F. J. Effects of partial perceptual isolation in mentally disturbed individuals. *Dis. nerv. Sys.* 1956, *17*, 117-122.

AZIMA, H. and Cramer, F. J. Studies on perceptual isolation. *Dis. nerv. Sys.*, 1957, *18*, 80-85.

AZIMA, H., and Wittkower, E. D. Gratification of basic needs in treatment of schizophrenia. *Psychiat.*, 1956, *19*, 121.

AZIMA, H., Wittkower, E. D., and Latendresse, J. Object relations therapy of schizophrenic states. *Amer. J. Psychiat.*, 1958, *115*, 60.

AZIMA, H., Vispo, R., and Azima, F. J. Observations on anaclitic therapy during sensory deprivation. In P. Solomon, et al. (Eds.), *Sensory deprivation*, Cambridge: Harvard Univers. Press, 1961, pp 142-160.

BERLYNE, D. E. *Conflict, arousal, and curiosity.* New York: McGraw-Hill, 1960.

BROWNFIELD, C. A. Deterioration and facilitation hypotheses in sensory deprivation research. *Psychol. Bull.*, 1964, *61*, 304-313. (a)

BROWNFIELD, C. A. Sensory deprivation: a comprehensive survey. *Psychologia*, 1964, *7*, 63-93. (b)

BROWNFIELD, C. A. *Isolation: clinical and experimental approaches.* New York: Random House, 1965.

BURNS, N. M., and Kimura, D. Isolation and sensory deprivation. In N. M. Burns, R. M. Chambers and E. Hendler (Eds.), *Unusual environments and human behavior.* New York: Free Press of Glencoe, 1963.

COHEN, S. I., Silverman, A. J., Bressler, B., and Shmavonian, B. M. Practical and theoretic difficulties in "isolation" studies. Paper presented at Office of Naval Research Symposium on Sensory Deprivation, Boston: June, 1958.

COOPER, G. D., Adams, H. B., and Gibby, R. G. Ego strength changes following perceptual deprivation. *Arch. gen. Psychiat.*, 1962, *7*, 213-217.

FISKE, D. W., and Maddi, S. R. A conceptual framework. In D. W. Fiske and S. R. Maddi (Eds.), *Functions of varied experience.* Homewood, Ill.: Dorsey Press, 1961, pp 11-56.

GIBBY, R. G. Adams, H. B., and Carrera, R. N. Therapeutic changes in psychiatric patients following partial sensory deprivation. *AMA Arch. gen. Psychiat.*, 1960, *3*, 33-42.

GOLDBERGER, I., and Holt, R. R. A comparison of isolation effects and their personality correlates in two divergent samples. *ASD Tech. Rep.* No. 61-417, 1961.

GOLDSTEIN, K. *The organism.* New York: American Book Co., 1939.

HARRIS, A. Sensory deprivation and schizophrenia. *J. ment. Sci.,* 1959, *105,* 235-237.

HEBB, D. O., and Thompson, W. R. The social significance of animal studies. In G. Lindzey (Ed.), *Handbook of social psychology.* Cambridge: Addison-Wesley, 1954, pp 551-552.

HOWARD, K. A. A test of stimulus-seeking behavior. *Percept. mot. Skills,* 1961, *13,* 416.

KUBZANSKY, P. E. The effects of reduced environmental stimulation on human behavior: a review. In A. D. Biderman and H. Zimmer (Eds.), *The manipulation of human behavior.* New York: John Wiley & Sons, 1961.

LEUBA, C. Toward some integration of learning theories: the concept of optimal stimulation. *Psychol. Rep.,* 1955, *1,* 27-33.

ROSENZWEIG, N. Sensory deprivation and schizophrenia: some clinical and theoretical similarities. *Amer. J. Psychiat.,* 1959, *116,* 326.

SCHULTZ, D. P. *Sensory restriction.* New York: Academic Press, 1965.

VERNON, J. A. *Inside the black room.* New York: Clarkson N. Potter, 1963.

WITKIN, H. A. Perception of body position and the position of the visual field. *Psychol. Monogr.,* 1949, *63* (Whole No. 7).

ZUCKERMAN, M. The development of an Affect Adjective Check List for the measurement of anxiety. *J. consult. Psychol.,* 1960, *24,* 457-462.

ZUCKERMAN, M., Albright, R. J., Marks, C. S., and Miller, G. L. Stress and hallucinatory effects of perceptual isolation and confinement. *Psychol. Monogr.,* 1962, *72* (Whole No. 549).

ZUCKERMAN, M. and Cohen, N. Sources of reports of visual and auditory sensations in perceptual isolation experiments. *Psychol. Bull.,* 1964, *62,* 1-20.

ZUCKERMAN, M., Kolin, E. A., Price, L., and Zoob, I. Development of a Sensation-Seeking Scale. *J. consult. Psychol.,* 1964, *28,* 477-482.

A Reference Bibliography
on Isolation Phenomena

This bibliography provides as comprehensive a listing as possible, as of the completion of this book, and includes articles and books relevant to the problems of isolation, sensory and perceptual deprivation, brainwashing, restricted early experience, feral man, and other related topics. Most of the references given here are covered in the body of this text, but some are not; these have come to the author's attention since the writing of the major part of this material or were in the process of publication while it was being written. They have been included here in the interest of greater comprehensiveness but with the recognition that in a broad, expanding field like isolation, impetus and momentum in research make it difficult to keep abreast of all the latest developments, and any such listing would be old by the time of publication. However, there is always a need on the part of researchers and students for reference lists in specific fields such as this one; and the following may be helpful for orientation purposes and as an aid to further research, study, and writing. While it is certainly not as inclusive as some might wish, this bibliography represents as complete a gathering of materials bearing directly on the topics touched in this book as has appeared in print to date. The emphasis, by count, is heaviest upon experimental sensory deprivation studies, but with a generous sprinkling of articles and books on related isolation phenomena. For the most part, studies focusing on a specific sense modality such as vision, audition, etc., have not been included. Those subjects, however, which specifically relate to experiments and issues evolving from the original McGill University studies, as well as topics such as brainwashing and human capabilities in space travel, which have been repeatedly associated with sensory deprivation, have been included. Some of the references are relevant by implication; of these, the choice was the author's and could conceivably have been better selected, but limitations in judgment and in space dictated what does appear here.

ADAMS, H. B., Carrera, R. N., Cooper, C. D., Gibby, R. G. and Tobey, H. R. Personality and intellectual changes in psychiatric patients following brief partial sensory deprivation. *Amer. Psychol.*, 1960, 15, 448 (abstract).

AI SSU-CHI. On problems of ideological reform. *Hsueh Hsi*, 1951, 3.

ALLPORT, F. H. *Theories of perception and the concept of structure.* New York: John Wiley & Sons, 1955.

ANONYMOUS. As minds grow misty. *Newsweek*, Nov. 23, 1959, 54, 60. (a)

ANONYMOUS. Sensory deprivation. *Lancet*, 1959, 2, 1072. (b)

ARBIT, J. Two early reports on the effects of sensory deprivation. *Amer. J. Psychiat.*, 1960, 117, 467–8.

ARNHOFF, F. N., and Leon, H. V. *Bibliography of sensory deprivation, isolation and confinement.* University of Miami, School of Medicine, Dept. of Psychiatry, August, 1962.

——. Personality factors related to success and failure

in sensory deprivation subjects. *Percept. Mot. Skills,* 1963, 16, 46. (a)

————. Sex differences in response to short-term sensory deprivation and isolation. *Percept. Mot. Skills,* 1963, 17, 81–2. (b)

ARNHOFF, F. N., Leon, H. V. and Brownfield, C. A. Sensory deprivation: its effects on human learning. *Science,* 1962, 138 (No. 3543), 899–900.

AZIMA, H., and Cramer, F. J. Effects of decrease in sensory variability on body scheme. *Canad. J. Psychiat.,* 1956, 1, 59–72. (a)

————. Effects of partial perceptual isolation in mentally disturbed individuals. *Dis. Nerv. Sys.,* 1956, 17, 117–22. (b)

AZIMA, H., and CRAMER-AZIMA, F. J. Studies on perceptual isolation. *Dis. Nerv. Sys.* (Monogr. Suppl.), 1957, 18, 80–5.

AZIMA, H., and Wittkower, E. D. Gratification of basic needs in treatment of schizophrenia. *Psychiatry,* 1956, 19, 121.

AZIMA, H., Wittkower, E. D. and Latendresse, J. Object relations therapy of schizophrenic states. *Amer. J. Psychiat.,* 1958, 115, 60.

AZIMA, H., Vispo, R. and Azima, F. J. Observations on anaclitic therapy during sensory deprivation. In P. Solomon *et al.* (Eds.), *Sensory Deprivation.* Cambridge: Harvard University Press, 1961, pp. 142–60.

AZIMA, H., Lemieux, M., and Azima, F. Isolement sensoriel, étude psychopathologique et psychanalytique de la régression et du schéma corporel. *L'évolution psychiatrique,* 1962, 2, 259–82.

BAKAN, D. An investigation of the effects of sensory deprivation on stall perception. *Abstracts of Doctoral Dissertations,* Ohio State University, 1949, 58, 29.

BAKAN, P. Discrimination decrement as a function of time in a prolonged vigil. *J. Exp. Psychol.,* 1955, 50, 387-90.

BAKER, C. H. Toward a theory of vigilance. *Canad. J. Psychol.,* 1959, 13, 35–42.

BAKWIN, H. Loneliness in infants. *Amer J. Dis. Child.,* 1942, 63, 30–40.

BARNARD, G. W., Wolff, H. D., and Graveline, D. E. Sensory deprivation under null gravity conditions. *Amer. J. Psychiat.,* 1962, 118, 921–5.

BARON, The (*pseudonym*). The girl in the leather mask: a suggestive study on sensory deprivation as a means to stimulate ESP phenomena. *Minute Scope,* 1963, 1 (No. 1), 14–15.

―――. The witches cradle and ESP: No. 2 in a series on sensory deprivation as a means to stimulate ESP phenomena. *Minute Scope,* 1964, 1 (No. 2), 14-15.

BARTLETT, J. E. A. A case of organized visual hallucinations in an old man with cataract and their relation to the phenomena of the phantom limb. *Brain,* 1951, 74, 363–73.

BARTLEY, S. N., and Chute, E. *Fatigue and impairment in man.* New York: McGraw-Hill, 1947.

BAUER, R. A. Brainwashing: psychology or demonology? *J. Soc. Issues,* 1957, 13, 41–7.

BAXTER, B. L. An electrophysiological study of effects of sensory deprivation. Unpublished doctoral dissertation, University of Chicago, 1959.

BECK, F., and GODIN, W. *Russian purge and the extraction of confessions.* Translated by Mosbacker, E., and Porter, D. New York: The Viking Press, 1951.

BEIGEL, H. G. The influence of body position on mental processes. *J. Clin. Psychol.,* 1952, 8, 193–9.

BENNETT, A. M. H. Sensory deprivation in aviation. *In* P. Solomon *et al.* (Eds.), *Sensory deprivation.* Cambridge: Harvard University Press, 1961.

BERNICOT, L. *The voyage of Anahita—single-handed round the world.* London: Rupert Hart-Davis, Soho Square, 1953.

BEXTON, W. H. Some effects of perceptual isolation on human subjects. Unpublished doctoral dissertation, McGill University, 1953.

BEXTON, W. H., Heron, W., and Scott, T. H. Effects of decreased variation in the sensory environment. *Canad. J. Psychol.,* 1954, 8, 70–6.

BIDERMAN, A. D. *Communist techniques of coercive interrogation.* Lackland AFB, Texas, Air Force Personnel and Training Research Center, December, 1956. AFPTRC *Development Report* TN-56-132.

―――. *Effects of Communist indoctrination attempts: some comments based on an Air Force prisoner-of-war study.* Washington, D.C.: Office of Intelligence Research, U. S. Dept. of State, Oct. 7, 1957. *External Research Paper* No. 132. (a)

————. Communist attempts to elicit false confessions from Air Force prisoners of war. *Bull. N.Y. Acad. Med.,* 1957, 33, 616–25. (b)

————. Effects of Communist indoctrination attempts: some comments based on an Air Force prisoner-of-war study. *Soc. Probl.,* 1959, 6, 304–13.

————. Social psychological needs and "involuntary" behavior as illustrated by compliance in interrogation. *Sociometry,* 1960, 23, 120–47.

BIDERMAN, A. D., and Monroe, J. L. Reactions to the Korean POW episode. A paper read at the annual Convention of the Amer. Psychol. Assn., Washington, D.C., September, 1958.

BIDERMAN, A. D., and Zimmer, H. (Eds.). *The manipulation of human behavior.* New York: John Wiley & Sons, 1961.

BOERNSTEIN, W. S. Visual images: induced hallucinations. *Trans. N.Y. Acad. Sci.,* 1957, 20, 72.

BOMBARD, A. *The voyage of the Hérétique.* New York: Simon and Schuster, 1953.

BONE, E. *Seven years' solitary.* New York: Harcourt Brace, 1957.

BOVARD, E. W. The effects of social stimuli on response to stress. *Psychol. Rev.,* 1959, 66, 267–77.

BRAINARD, D. L. *The outpost of the lost: an arctic adventure.* Indianapolis: Bobbs-Merrill, 1929.

BROADBENT, D. E. Classical conditioning and human watchkeeping. *Psychol. Rev.,* 1953, 60, 331–9.

————. *Perception and communication.* New York: Pergamon Press, 1958, Ch. 6.

BROWN, J. L. (Ed.). Sensory and perceptual problems related to space flight. (NAS-NRC Publ. 872.) Washington, D.C.: National Academy of Sciences-National Research Council, 1961.

BROWNFIELD, C. A. Behavioral rigidity; the 'Einstellung' phenomenon in a delinquent population. *J. Correctional Ed.,* 1963, 15 (No. 2), 10-12.

————. Deterioration and facilitation hypotheses in sensory deprivation research. *Psychol. Bull.,* 1964, 61, 304–13.

————. Formation and dissolution of the 'Einstellung' phenomenon in a delinquent population. *J. Clin. Psychol.,* 1964, 20, 74–9.

————. Sensory deprivation: a comprehensive survey. *Psychologia,* 1964, 7, 63–93.

BROZEK, J. Psychology of human starvation and nutritional rehabilitation. *Scient. Monogr.*, 1950, 70, 270–4.

———. Nutrition and behavior; psychologic changes in acute starvation with hard physical work. *J. Amer. Diet. Assn.*, 1955, 31, 703–7.

BRUNER, J. S. The cognitive consequences of early sensory deprivation. *Psychosom. Med.*, 1959, 21, 89–95.

BURNEY, C. *Solitary confinement.* New York: Coward-McCann, 1952.

BUTLER, R. A. The effect of deprivation of visual incentives on visual exploration motivation in monkeys. *J. Comp. Physiol. Psychol.*, 1957, 50, 177–9.

BYRD, R. E. *Alone.* New York: G. P. Putnam's Sons, 1938.

CAMBERARI, J. D. The effects of sensory isolation on suggestible and non-suggestible psychology graduate students. Unpublished doctoral dissertation, University of Utah, 1958.

CAMERON, D. E., Levy, L., Ban, T., and Rubenstein, L. Sensory deprivation: effects upon the functioning brain in space systems. *In* B. E. Flaherty (Ed.), *Psychophysiological aspects of space flight.* New York: Columbia University Press, 1961, 225–37.

CHILES, W. D. Experimental studies of prolonged wakefulness. *USAF WADC Tech. Rep.*, 1955, 55–395.

CLARK, B., and Graybiel, A. The "breakoff" phenomenon: a feeling of separation from earth experienced by pilots at high altitudes. *J. Aviat. Med.*, 1957, 28, 121.

CLEVELAND, S. E., Reitman, E. E., and Bentinck, C. Therapeutic effectiveness of sensory deprivation. *Arch. Gen. Psychiat.*, 1963, 8, 455–60.

COHEN, B. D., Rosenbaum, G., Dobie, S. I., and Gottlieb, J. S. Sensory isolation: hallucinogenic effects of a brief procedure. *J. Nerv. Ment. Dis.*, 1959, 129, 486–91.

COHEN, S. I., Silverman, A. J., Bressler, B., and Shmavonian, B. M. Practical and theoretic difficulties in "isolation" studies. Paper presented at ONR Symposium on Sensory Deprivation, Boston, Mass., June, 1958.

COHEN, W. *Some perceptual and physiological aspects of uniform visual stimulation.* Washington, D.C.; Research and Development Division, Office of the Surgeon General, Dept. of the Army, 1958, *Progress Report* No. 1.

COLLIER, R. M. (Reviewer). The more intense phenomenology (a review of L. J. West's [Ed.] *Hallucinations*). *Contemp. Psychol.*, 1963, 8, 316–17.

COOPER, G. D., Adams, H. B., and Gibby, R. G. Ego strength changes following perceptual deprivation. *Arch. Gen. Psychiat.*, 1962, 7, 213–17.

COURTAULD, A. Living alone under polar conditions. *The Polar Record*, 1932, No. 4, Cambridge, Mass.: Harvard University Press.

COURTNEY, J., Davis, J. M., and Solomon, P. Sensory deprivation: the role of movement. *Percept. Mot. Skills*, 1961, 13, 191–9.

CROFT, F. Look what utter boredom can do. *Maclean's Magazine*, 1954, 67, 18–19, 88–90.

DAVIS, J. M., McCourt, W. F., and Solomon, P. Sensory deprivation: (1) effects on social contact, (2) effects of random visual stimulation. Paper presented at Amer. Psychiat. Assn. Meeting, Philadelphia, April, 1959.

———. The effect of visual stimulation on hallucinations and other mental experiences during sensory deprivation. *Amer. J. Psychiat.*, 1960, 116, 889–92.

DAVIS, J. M., McCourt, W. F., Courtney, J., and Solomon, P. Sensory deprivation: the role of social isolation. *Arch. Gen. Psychiat.*, 1961, 5, 84–90.

DAVIS, K. Extreme social isolation of a child. *Amer. J. Sociol.*, 1940, 1, 554–65.

———. Final note on a case of extreme isolation. *Amer. J. Sociol.*, 1947, 52, 432–7.

DAVIS, R. C. Somatic activity under reduced stimulation. *J. Comp. Physiol. Psychol.*, 1959, 52, 309–14.

DEAN, W. F. *General Dean's story.* New York: The Viking Press, 1954.

DEMENT, W. The effect of dream deprivation. *Science*, 1960, 131, 1705–07.

DEMPSEY, C. A., Van Wart, E. D., Duddy, J. H., and Hockenberry, J. Long-term human confinement in space equivalent vehicles. *Trans. Amer. Astronautical Soc.*, 1957, 88–93.

DENNIS, W. Infant development under conditions of restricted practice and of minimum social stimulation: a preliminary report. *J. Genet. Psychol.*, 1938, 53, 149–57.

———. Infant development under conditions of restricted practice and of minimum social stimulation. *Genet. Psychol. Monogr.*, 1941, 23, 143–89.

DENNIS, W. and Dennis, M. G. The effect of cradling practices upon the onset of walking in Hopi children. *J. Genet. Psychol.*, 1940, 56, 77–86.

————. Development under controlled environmental conditions. *In* W. Dennis (Ed.), *Readings in child psychology.* New York: Prentice-Hall, 1951.

DICKENS, C. *American notes and pictures of Italy.* Chapt. VII, "Philadelphia and its Solitary Prison," Gadskill edition, New York: Chas. Scribner & Sons, 1898.

DOANE, B. K. Changes in visual function with perceptual isolation. Unpublished doctoral dissertation, McGill University, 1955.

DOANE, B. K., Mahatoo, W., Heron, W., and Scott, T. H. Changes in perceptual function after isolation. *Canad. J. Psychol.*, 1959, 13, 210–19.

EILBERT, L. R., Glaser, R., and Hanes, R. M. Research on the feasibility of selection of personnel for duty at isolation stations. USAF Personnel Training Research Center, Lackland Air Force Base, San Antonio, Texas. *Tech. Rep.* No. 57–4, 1957 (July).

ELLAM, P., and Mudie, C. *Sopranino,* New York: W. W. Norton, 1953.

EVANS, B. The wolf child. *New Republic,* 1941, 104, 892. (a)

————. Wolf! Wolf! *New Republic,* 1941, 104, 734–5. (b)

EVANS, E. E. *The story of Kaspar Hauser from authentic records.* London, 1892.

FARBER, I. E., Harlow, H. F., and West, L. J. Brainwashing, conditioning and DDD (debility, dependency and dread). *Sociometry,* 1957, 20, 271–85.

FEDERN, E. The endurance of torture. *Complex,* 1951, 4, 34–41.

FEUERBACH, Ritter von (Paul Johann Anselm). *Caspar Hauser.* Translated by H. G. Linberg. Boston, Allen and Ticknor, 1832.

FISKE, D. W. Effects of monotonous and restricted stimulation. *In* D. W. Fiske and S. R. Maddi (Eds.), *Functions of varied experience.* Homewood, Ill.: Dorsey Press, 1961, 106–44.

FISKE, D. W., and Maddi, S. R. (Eds.). *Functions of varied experience.* Homewood, Ill.: Dorsey Press, 1961.

FLYNN, W. R. Visual hallucinations in sensory deprivation. *Psychiat. Quart.,* 1962, 36, 55–65.

FRANCIS, R. D. The effect of prior instructions and time

knowledge on tolerance of sensory isolation. *J. Nerv. Ment. Dis.*, 1964, **139**, 182–5.

FRANKLIN, J. C., Schiele, B. C., Brozek, J., and Keyse, A. Observations on human behavior in experimental semistarvation and rehabilitation. *J. Clin. Psychol.*, 1948, **4**, 28–45.

FREEDMAN, S. J. Perceptual changes in sensory deprivation: suggestions for a conative theory. *J. Nerv. Ment. Dis.*, 1961, **132**, 17–21.

FREEDMAN, S. J., and Greenblatt, M. Studies in human isolation. *WADC Tech. Rep.* 59–266, USAF, Wright-Patterson AFB, Ohio, 1959.

FREEDMAN, S. J., and Held, R. Sensory deprivation and perceptual lag. *Percept. Mot. Skills*, 1960, **11**, 277–80.

FREEDMAN, S. J., Gruenbaum, H., Stare, F. A., and Greenblatt, M. Imagery in sensory deprivation. *In* L. J. West (Ed.), *Hallucinations*. New York: Grune & Stratton, 1962.

FRENCH, J. D. The reticular formation. *Sci. Amer.*, 1957, **196**, 54–60.

FREUD, A., and Burlingham, D. *Infants without families.* New York: International Universities Press, 1944.

FRISCH, B. H. Solitude: who can take it and who can't. *Science Digest*, 1964 (March), **55** (no. 3), 12–18.

GADDIS, T. E. *Birdman of Alcatraz: the story of Robert Stroud.* New York: Signet Books, 1958.

GESELL, A. *Wolf child and human child.* London: Methuen, 1941.

GIBBY, R. G., Adams, H. B., and Carrera, R. N. Therapeutic changes in psychiatric patients following partial sensory deprivation. *AMA Arch. Gen. Psychiat.*, 1960, **3**, 33–42.

GIBSON, W. *The boat.* Boston: Houghton Mifflin (Riverside Press), 1953.

GLANZER, M. Curiosity, exploratory drive and stimulus satiation. *Psychol. Bull.*, 1958, **55**, 302–15.

GOLDBERG, I. The effects of sensory deprivation on intellectual efficiency as a function of personality. *Dissertation Abstracts*, 1961, **21**, 2797.

GOLDBERGER, L. Individual differences in effects of perceptual isolation as related to Rorschach manifestations of primary process. *Dissertation Abstracts*, 1959, **19**, 1816–17.

———. Homogeneous visual stimulation (Ganzfeld) and imagery. *Perceptual Mot. Skills*, 1961, **12**, 91–3.

GOLDBERGER, L., and Holt, R. R. Experimental interference

with reality contact (perceptual isolation): method and group results. *J. Nerv. Ment. Dis.,* 1958, **127**, 99–112. (a)

——. Experimental interference with reality contact (perceptual isolation). *J. Nerv. Ment. Dis.,* 1958, **127**, 112. (b)

——. A comparison of isolation effects and their personality correlates in two divergent samples. *ASD Tech. Rep.* No. 61-417, 1961.

GOLDFARB, W. The effects of early institutional care on adolescent personality. *J. Exper. Educ.,* 1943, **12**, 106–29.

——. Effects of early institutional care on adolescent personality: Rorschach data. *Amer. J. Orthopsychiat.,* 1944, **14**, 441–7. (a)

——. Infant rearing as a factor in foster home placement. *Amer. J. Orthopsychiat.,* 1944, **14**, 162–7. (b)

GOLDFRIED, M. R. A psychoanalytic interpretation of sensory deprivation. *Psychol. Rec.,* 1960, **10**, 211–14.

GRISSOM, R. J., Suedfeld, P., and Vernon, J. Memory for verbal material: effects of sensory deprivation. *Science,* 1962, **138**, 429–30.

Group for the Advancement of Psychiatry. *Factors used to increase the susceptibility of individuals to forceful indoctrination: observations and experiments.* GAP Symposium No. 3. New York: GAP Publications Office, December, 1956.

——. *Methods of forceful indoctrination: observations and interviews.* GAP Symposium No. 4. New York: GAP Publications Office, July, 1957.

GRUENBAUM, H. V., Freedman, S. J., and Greenblatt, M. Sensory deprivation and personality. *Amer. J. Psychiat.,* 1960, **116**, 878–82.

HACKER, A. Dostoevsky's disciples: man and sheep in political theory. *J. Politics,* 1955, **18**, 590–613.

HARING, J. Preface (to special issue on "Brainwashing"). *J. Soc. Issues,* 1957, **13**, 1–2.

HARLOW, H. F. Mice, monkeys, men, and motives. *Psychol. Rev.,* 1953, **60**, 23–32.

——. The nature of love. *Amer. Psychologist,* 1958, **13**, 673–85.

——. The heterosexual affectional system in monkeys. *Amer. Psychologist,* 1962, **17**, 1–9.

HARLOW, H. F., and Zimmerman, R. R. Affectional responses in the infant monkey. *J. Comp. Physio. Psychol.,* 1954, **47**, 73.

HARRIS, A. Sensory deprivation and schizophrenia. *J. Ment. Sci.,* 1959, **105**, 235–7.

HATCH, A., Wilberg, G. S., Balazs, T., and Grice, H. C. Long-term isolation stress in rats. *Science,* 1963, **142**, 507.

HEBB, D. O. *The organization of behavior.* New York: John Wiley & Sons, 1949.

———. The mammal and his environment. *Amer. J. Psychol.,* 1955, **111**, 826–31.

———. The motivating effects of exteroceptive stimulation. *Amer. Psychologist,* 1958, **13**, 109.

———. Sensory deprivation: facts in search of a theory. *J. Nerv. Ment. Dis.,* 1961, **132**, 40–3.

———. The semiautonomous process: its nature and nurture. *Amer. Psychologist,* 1963, **18**, 16–27.

HEBB, D. O., Heath, E. S., and Stuart, E. A. Experimental deafness. *Canad. J. Psychol.,* 1954, **8**, 152–6.

HELD, R. Sensory deprivation: facts in search of a theory: exposure history as a factor in maintaining stability of perception and coordination. *J. Nerv. Ment. Dis.,* 1961, **132**, 26–32.

HELD, R., and White, B. Sensory deprivation and visual speed: an analysis. *Science,* 1959, **130**, 860–1.

HELSON, H. Adaptation level as frame of reference for prediction of psychological data. *Amer. J. Psychol.,* 1947, **60**, 1–29.

———. Adaptation level as a basis for a quantitative theory of frames of reference. *Psychol. Rev.,* 1948, **55**, 297–313.

HERNANDEZ-PEON, R., Scherrer, H., and Jouvet, M. Modification of electric activity in cochlear nucleus during attention in unanesthetized cats. *Science,* 1956, **123**, 331–2.

HERON, W. The pathology of boredom. *Sci. Amer.,* 1957, **196**, 52–6.

———. Cognitive and physiological effects of perceptual isolation. *In* P. Solomon *et al.* (Eds.), *Sensory deprivation.* Cambridge, Mass.: Harvard University Press, 1961, 6–36.

HERON, W., Bexton, W. H., and Hebb, D. O. Cognitive effects of decreased variation to sensory environment. *Amer. Psychologist,* 1953, **8**, 366 (abstract).

HERON, W., Doane, B. K., and Scott, T. H. Visual disturbances after prolonged perceptual isolation. *Canad. J. Psychol.,* 1956, **10**, 13–18.

HILL, J. C., and Robinson, B. A case of retarded mental development associated with restricted movements in infancy. *Brit. J. Med.,* 1929, 268–77.

HILL, K. T., and Stevenson, H. W. Effectiveness of social reinforcement following social and sensory deprivation. *J. Abnorm. Soc. Psychol.,* 1964, **68,** 579–84.

HINKLE, L. E., Jr. *In* Group for the Advancement of Psychiatry, *Methods of forceful indoctrination: observations and interviews.* New York: GAP Publications Office, July, 1957, GAP Symposium No. 4, 285–92.

HINKLE, L. E., Jr. and Wolff, H. G. Communist interrogation and indoctrination of "Enemies of the State." Analysis of methods used by the Communist state police. (Special Report) *AMA Arch. Neurol. Psychiat.,* 1956, **76,** 115–74.

————. The methods of interrogation used by Communist state police. *Bull. N.Y. Acad. Med.,* 1957, **33,** 600–15. (a)

————. The nature of man's adaptation to his total environment and the relation of this to illness. *AMA Arch. Int. Med.,* 1957, **99,** 442–60. (b)

HOCHBERG, J., Triebel, W., and Seaman, G. Color adaptation under conditions of homogeneous visual stimulation (Ganzfeld). *J. Exp. Psychol.,* 1951, 41, 153–9.

HOLT, R. R., and Goldberger, L. Personological correlates of reactions to perceptual isolation. USAF, *WADC Tech. Rep.* No. 59-735, 1959.

————. Research on the effects of isolation on cognitive functioning. USAF, *WADC Tech. Rep.* No. 60-260, 1960.

————. Assessment of individual resistance to sensory alteration. *In* B. E. Flaherty (Ed.), *Psychophysiological aspects of space flight.* New York: Columbia Univer. Press, 1961, 248–62.

HRDRICKA, A. *Children who run on all fours.* New York: Harper & Brothers, 1941.

HULL, J., and Zubek, J. P. Personality characteristics of successful and unsuccessful sensory isolation subjects. *Percept. Mot. Skills,* 1962, 14, 231–40.

HULTGREN, H. P. Prisoners of war: clinical and laboratory observations in severe starvation. *Stanford Med. Bull.,* 1951, 9, 175–91.

HUNTER, E. *Brainwashing in Red China.* New York: Vanguard Press, 1953.

————. *Brainwashing: the story of men who defied it.* New York: Farrar, Straus and Cudahy, 1956.

HUTTON, J. H. Wolf children. *Folk Lore*, 1940, 51, 9–31.
HUXLEY, A. *The Devils of Loudun.* New York: Harper & Brothers, 1952.
————. *Brave new world revisited.* New York: Harper & Brothers, 1958.
INSTITORES (H. Draemer), and Sprenger, J. *Malleus Maleficarum.* Translated by Montague Summers. London: J. Rodker, 1928.
ITARD, J. M. G. *The wild boy of Aveyron,* translated by George and Muriel Humphrey. New York: Appleton-Century-Crofts, 1932.
JACKSON, C. W., Jr. An exploratory study of the role of suggestion in research on sensory deprivation. Unpublished doctoral dissertation, University of Michigan, 1960.
JACKSON, C. W., Jr., and Kelly, E. L. Influence of suggestion and subjects' prior knowledge in research on sensory deprivation. *Science,* 1962, 135, 211–12.
JACKSON, C. W., and Pollard, J. C. Sensory deprivation and suggestion: a theoretical approach. *Behav. Sci.,* 1962, 7, 332–42.
JACKSON, C. W., Pollard, J. C., and Kansky, E. W. The application of findings from experimental sensory deprivation to cases of clinical sensory deprivation. *Amer. J. Sci.,* 1962, 243, 558–63.
JAMES, W. *The varieties of religious experience.* New York: Doubleday, 1902.
JANIS, I. L. *Are the Cominform countries using hypnotic techniques to elicit confessions in public trials?* Santa Monica, California: RAND Corp., April 25, 1949, RM 161.
JASPER, H. Reticular-cortical systems and theories of the integrative action of the brain. *In* Harlow and Woolsey (Eds.), *Biological and biochemical bases of behavior.* Madison: University of Wisconsin Press, 1958, 57–8.
JONES, H. E. Problems of aging in perceptive and intellective functions. *In* Anderson, J. E. (Ed.), *Psychological aspects of aging.* Washington, D.C.: APA, 1956, 135–9.
JORDAN, H. You too would confess. *Argosy,* February, 1957, 15–17, 57–63.
KANDEL, E. J., Meyers, T. I., and Murphy, D. B. Influence of prior verbalization and instructions on visual sensations reported under conditions of reduced sensory input. *Amer. Psychologist,* 1958, 13, 344 (abstract).
KARDINER, A. Traumatic neuroses of war. *In* Arieti, S. (Ed.),

American handbook of psychiatry. New York: Basic Books, 1959.

KELLER, M. J. Bimodal effects of sensory deprivation. *Dissert. Abstr.,* 1963, **23,** 2593 (abstract).

KELLOGG, W. N. A further note on the "wolf-children" of India. *Amer. J. Psychol.,* 1934, **46,** 149–50.

KENNAWAY, J. *The mind benders.* New York: Atheneum, 1963.

KING, J. A. Parameters relevant to determining the effects of early experience upon adult behavior of animals. *Psychol. Bull.,* 1958, **55,** 46–58.

KINKEAD, E. A. A study of something new in history. *New Yorker,* 1957, **26,** (Oct.).

———. *In every war but one.* New York: W. W. Norton, 1959.

KITAMURA, S. Studies on sensory deprivation I. I: Introduction. *Tohoku Psychologia Folia,* 1963, **22,** 1–4.

KRAL, V. A. Psychiatric observations under chronic stress. *Amer. J. Psychiat.,* 1951, **108,** 185.

KRIVITZKY, W. G. *In Stalin's secret service.* New York: Harper & Brothers, 1939.

KUBIE, L. S. The value of induced dissociated states in the therapeutic process. *Proc. No. 7, Soc. Med.,* 1954, London, **38,** 681.

KUBZANSKY, P. E. The effects of reduced environmental stimulation on human behavior; a review. *In* A. D. Biderman and H. Zimmer (Eds.), *The manipulation of human behavior.* New York: John Wiley & Sons, 1961, 51–95.

KUBZANSKY, P. E., and Leiderman, P. M. Sensory deprivation: an overview. *In* P. Solomon *et al.* (Eds.), *Sensory deprivation.* Cambridge: Harvard University Press, 1961, 221–38.

KUBZANSKY, P. E., Leiderman, P. M., Mendelson, J., Wexler, D., and Solomon, P. A comparison of two conditions of sensory deprivation. Paper presented at *Amer. Psychol. Assn.,* Washington, D.C., Sept., 1958.

LAWES, T. G. Schizophrenia, "Sernyl," and sensory deprivation. *Brit. J. Psychol.,* 1963, **109** (Whole No. 459), 243–50.

LEIDERMAN, P. M. Man alone: sensory deprivation and behavioral change. *Corr. Psychiat. and J. Soc. Therapy,* 1962, **8,** 64–74.

LEIDERMAN, P. M., Mendelson, J. E., Wexler, D., Kubzansky,

P. E., and Solomon, P. *Sensory deprivation: clinical aspects.* Report No. 3, Naval Res. Grant 1866 (29), Cambridge, Mass. *Dept. Psychiat.,* 1954, 732–9.

LEON, H. V. Cognitive and perceptual disturbances in sensory deprivation as a function of differential expectancy levels. Unpublished master's thesis, University of Miami, 1963.

LERMOLO, E. *Face of a victim.* Translated from the Russian by I. D. W. Talmage. New York: Harper & Brothers, 1955.

LEVY, D. M. On the problem of movement restraint. *Amer. J. Orthopsychiat.,* 1944, 14, 644–71.

LEVY, E. Z. The subjects' approach: important factor in experimental isolation. *Bull. Menninger Clin.,* 1962, 26, 30–42.

LEVY, E., Ruff, G., and Thaler, V. Studies in human isolation. *J. Amer. Med. Assn.,* 1959, 169, 236–9.

LIFTON, R. J. Home by ship: reaction patterns of American prisoners of war repatriated from North Korea. *Amer. J. Psychiat.,* 1954, 110, 732–9.

———. "Thought reform" of western civilians in Chinese Communist prisons. *Psychiatry,* 1956, 19, 173–95. (a)

———. *Chinese Communist "thought reform": "confession" and "re-education" in penal institutions.* Res. Devel. Div., Office of the Surgeon General, Dept. of the Army, 1956. (b)

LILLY, J. C. Mental effects of reduction of ordinary levels of physical stimuli on intact, healthy persons. American Psychiatric Association, *Psychiatric Research Reports,* 1956 (No. 5).

LILLY, J. C., Hughes, J. R., Alvord, E. C., Jr., and Galkin, T. W. Brief noninjurious electric waveform for stimulation of the brain. *Science,* 1955, 121, 468–9.

LILLY, J. C., and Shurley, J. T. Experiments in solitude in maximum achievable physical isolation with water suspension of intact, healthy person. Paper read, in part, at the Symposium on Sensory Deprivation, Harvard University Medical School, Boston, 1958.

LINDSLEY, D. B. Common factors in sensory deprivation, sensory distortion and sensory overload. *In* P. Solomon *et al.* (Eds.), *Sensory deprivation.* Cambridge: Harvard University Press, 1961, 174–94.

MACKWORTH, N. H. Researches on the measurement of

human performance. London: *Spec. Rep. Ser. Med. Res. Coun.*, 1950 (No. 268).

MAGOUN, H. W. An ascending reticular activating system in the brain. *AMA Arch. Neurol. and Psychiat.*, 1952, **67**, 145.

———. Non-specific brain mechanisms. *In* Harlow and Woolsey (Eds.), *Biological and biochemical bases of behavior.* Madison: University of Wisconsin Press, 1958.

MANDELBAUM, D. G. Wolf-child histories from India. *J. Soc. Psychol.*, 1943, **17**, 25–44.

MAYER, W. E. Why did so many GI captives cave in? *U.S. News and World Report*, February 24, 1956, 56–62.

MAYO, C. W. Destroying American minds—Russians made it a science. *U.S. News and World Report*, November 6, 1953, 97–101.

McGRATH, J. J., Harabedian, A., and Buckner, D. N. *Review and critique of the literature on vigilance performance.* Los Angeles: Human Factors Research, Inc., 1959.

MEERLOO, J. A. M. The crime of menticide. *Amer. J. Psychiat.*, 1951, **197**, 594–8.

———. Menticide. *In* Meerloo, *Conversation and communication.* New York: International Universities Press, 1952, 149–57.

———. Thought control and confession compulsion. *In* R. M. Lindner (Ed.), *Explorations in psychoanalysis.* New York: Julian Press, 1953, 28–37.

———. Pavlovian strategy as a weapon of menticide. *Amer. J. Psychiat.*, 1954, **110**, 173–96.

———. Medication into submission: the danger of therapeutic coercion. *J. Nerv. Ment. Dis.*, 1955, **122**, 353–60.

———. *The rape of the mind.* Cleveland: World Publishing Co., 1956.

MELTZER, M. Solitary confinement. *In* Group for the Advancement of Psychiatry. *Factors used to increase the susceptibility of individuals to forceful indoctrination: observations and experiments.* New York: GAP Publications Office, 1956, GAP Symposium No. 3, 960103, 96–103.

MELZACK, R. The genesis of emotional behavior. *J. Comp. Physiol. Psychol.*, 1954, **47**, 166–8.

MELZACK, R., and Scott, T. H. The effects of early experience on the response to pain. *J. Comp. Physiol. Psychol.*, 1957, **50**, 155.

MENDELSON, J., and Foley, J. M. Abnormality of mental function affecting patients with poliomyelitis in a tank type respirator. *Trans. Amer. Neurol. Assn.*, 1956, **81**, 134–8.

MENDELSON, J., DuToit, C., Liederman, P. M., Wexler, D., Marcottz, A., Kubzansky, P. E., and Solomon, P. The effects of sensory deprivation on epinephrine and nor-epinephrine excretion in man. Paper presented at Amer. Psychosom. Soc., Cincinnati, March, 1958.

MENDELSON, J., Solomon, P., and Lindemann, E. Hallucinations of poliomyelitis patients during treatment in a respirator. *J. Nerv. Ment. Dis.*, 1958, **126**, 421–8.

MENDELSON, J., Kubzansky, P., Leiderman, P. M., Wexler, D., DuToit, C., and Solomon, P. Catecholamine excretion and behavior during sensory deprivation. *AMA Arch. Psychiat.*, 1960, **2**, 147.

MERRIEN, J. *The lonely voyagers.* New York: G. P. Putnam's Sons, 1954.

MERTON, T. *The seeds of contemplation.* New York: Dell, 1960.

———. *The silent life.* New York: Dell, 1961.

MEYER, J. S., Greifenstein, F., and Devault, M. A new drug causing symptoms of sensory deprivation. *J. Nerv. Ment. Dis.*, 1959, **129**, 54–61.

MEYERS, A. K., and Miller, N. E. Failure to find a learned drive based on hunger; evidence for learning motivated by "exploration." *J. Comp. Physiol. Psychol.*, 1954, **47**, 428–36.

MILLER, J. G. Brainwashing: present and future. *J. Soc. Issues*, 1957, **13**, 48–55.

Misconduct in the prison camp: a survey of the law and an analysis of the Korean cases: a student note. *Columbia Law Rev.*, 1956, **56**, 709–94.

MONTGOMERY, K. C. The role of exploratory drive in learning. *J. Comp. Physiol. Psychol.*, 1954, **47**, 60–4.

MONTGOMERY, K. C., and Zimbardo, P. G. The effect of sensory and behavioral deprivation upon exploratory behavior in the rat. *Percept. Mot. Skills*, 1957, **7**, 223–9.

MORUZZI, G., and Magoun, H. W. Brain stem reticular formation and activation of the EEG. *Electroenceph. and Clin. Neurophysiol.*, 1949, **1**, 455–73.

MURPHY, C. W., and Cleghorn, R. A. The effects of perceptual deprivation on corticoid excretions in the urine. Unpublished paper cited in T. H. Scott's dissertation, McGill University, 1954.

MURPHY, D. B., Myers, T. I., and Smith, S. Reported visual sensations as a function of sustained sensory deprivation and social isolation. Pioneer VI Draft Research Report, U.S. Army Leadership Human Research Unit, California, 1962.

MURRAY, J. C. Singing is for the birds. *The Army Combat Forces J.*, 1955, 6, 15–21.

MYERS, T. I., Forbes, L. M., Arbit, J., and Hicks, J. *A preliminary study of the effects of controlled isolation.* Fort Ord, California, U.S. Army Leadership Human Research Unit, Feb., 1957.

MYERS, T. I., Murphy, D. B., and Smith, S. Progress report on studies of sensory deprivation. Presidio of Monterey, Calif., U.S. Army Leadership Human Research Unit, March, 1961.

MYERS, T. I., Murphy, D. B., Smith, S. and Windle, C. *Experimental assessment of a limited sensory and social environment: summary of the HUMRRO program.* Presidio of Monterey, Calif., U.S. Army Leadership Human Research Unit, Feb. 1962.

MYERS, T. I., and Murphy, D. B. Reported visual sensation during brief exposure to reduced sensory input. *In* L. J. West (Ed.), *Hallucinations.* New York: Grune & Stratton, 1962, 118–24.

NAGATSUKA, Y., and Maruyama, K. Studies on sensory deprivation I. II: Effects of sensory deprivation upon perceptual and motor functions. *Tohoku Psychologia Folia*, 1963, 22, 5–13.

OHKUBO, Y. Studies on sensory deprivation I. IV: Word association test. *Tohoku Psychologia Folia*, 1963, 22, 37–9.

OLDS, J. A physiological study of reward. In D. C. McClelland (Ed.), *Studies in motivation.* New York: Appleton-Century-Crofts, 1955, 134–43.

———. Self-stimulation of the brain: its use to study local effects of hunger, sex and drugs. *Science*, 1958, 127, 315–24.

ORMISTON, D. W. The effects of sensory deprivation and sensory bombardment on apparent movement thresholds. Unpublished doctoral dissertation. Purdue University, 1958. (*Dissertation Abstr.*, 1958, 18, 2200–1.) (a)

———. The effects of sensory deprivation and sensory bombardment on apparent movement thresholds. *Amer. Psychol.*, 1958, 13, 389 (Abstract). (b)

———. A methodological study of confinement. *Tech. Rep.*

61-258, Wright-Patterson AFB, Ohio, *WADC,* Aeromedical Lab., 1961.

ORNE, M. T. On the social psychology of the psychological experiment: with particular reference to demand characteristics and their implications. *Amer. Psychol.,* 1962, **17,** 776–83.

ORWELL, G. *Nineteen Eighty-Four.* New York: Harcourt Brace, 1949.

PACKARD, V. *The hidden persuaders.* New York: David McKay, 1957.

PARRY, A. Here come the cosmonauts: behind the scenes of Russia's man into space program. *Sci. Digest,* 1960, **48,** 23–8.

PENÁ, F. Perceptual isolation and hypnotic susceptibility. Unpublished doctoral dissertation, Washington State Univer., 1963.

PENFIELD, W., and Rasmussen, T. *The cerebral cortex of man: a clinical study of localization of function.* New York: Macmillan, 1950.

PETERS, J., Benjamin, F. B., Helvey, W. M., and Albright, G. A. Study of sensory deprivation, pain, and personality relationships for space travel. *Aerospace Med.,* 1963, **34,** 830–7.

PETERSON, D. B. Prisoners swayed didn't fall: Communists "sold" very few, says top Army psychiatrist. *U.S. News and World Report,* August 28, 1953, **35,** 28.

PETRIE, A., Collins, W., and Solomon, P. Pain sensitivity, sensory deprivation and susceptibility to satiation. *Science,* 1958, **128,** 1431.

———. The tolerance for pain and for sensory deprivation. *Amer. J. Psychol.,* 1960, **73,** 89–90.

POLLARD, J. C., Bakker, C., Uhr, L., and Feuerfile, D. F. Controlled sensory input. *Comprehen. Psychiat.,* 1960, **1,** 377–80.

POLLARD, J. C., Jackson, C. W., Jr., Uhr, L. and Feuerfile, D. F. A bibliography of experimental studies of sensory deprivation with human subjects. Mental Health Research Institute, University of Michigan, *Rep. No.* 11, 1961.

POLLARD, J. C., Uhr, L., and Jackson, C. W., Jr. Some unexpected findings in experimental sensory deprivation: the psychopharmacologic interaction of a placebo-potentiated suggestion. Paper read at American Psychological Association convention, St. Louis, 1963.

————. Studies in sensory deprivation. *Arch. Gen. Psychiat.*, 1963, **8**, 435–54.

PRUGH, G. S., Jr. Justice for all RECAP-K's. *The Army Combat Forces J.*, 1955, **6**, 15–26.

REITMAN, E., and Cleveland, S. E. Changes in body image following sensory deprivation in schizophrenic and control groups. *J. Abnorm. Soc. Psychol.*, 1964, **68**, 168–76.

RIESEN, A. H. The development of visual perception in man and chimpanzee. *Science*, 1947, **106**, 107.

————. Sensory deprivation: facts in search of a theory: studying perceptual development using the technique of sensory deprivation. *J. Nerv. Ment. Dis.*, 1961, **132**, 21–5. (a)

————. Stimulation as a requirement for growth and function in behavioral development. *In* D. W. Fiske and S. R. Maddi (Eds.), *Functions of varied experience.* Homewood, Ill.: Dorsey Press, 1961, 57–80. (b)

RIESMAN, D. Some observations on the limits of totalitarian power. *Antioch Rev.*, 1952, **12**, 155–68.

RIPIN, R. A comparative study of the development of infants in an institution with those in homes of low socioeconomic status. *Psychol. Bull.*, 1933, **30**, 680–1.

RITTER, C. *A woman in the polar night.* New York: E. P. Dutton, 1954.

ROBERTSON, M. H. Theoretical implications of sensory deprivation. *Psychol. Rec.*, 1961, **11**, 33–42.

ROBERTSON, M. H. and Wolter, D. J. The effect of sensory deprivation upon scores on the Wechsler Adult Intelligence Scale. *J. Psychol.*, 1963, **56**, 213–18.

ROLIN, J. *Police drugs.* Translated by L. J. Bendit. New York: Philosophical Library, 1956.

ROSENBAUM, G., Dobie, S. I., and Cohen, B. P. Visual recognition thresholds following sensory deprivation. *Amer. J. Psychol.*, 1959, **72**, 429–33.

ROSENZWEIG, N. Sensory deprivation and schizophrenia: some clinical and theoretical similarities. *Amer. J. Psychiat.*, 1959, **116**, 326.

ROSSI, A. M., Sturrock, J. B., and Solomon, P. Suggestion effects on reported imagery in sensory deprivation. *Percept. Mot. Skills*, 1963, **16**, 39–45.

ROSSI, A. M., and Solomon, P. Button-pressing for a time-off reward during sensory deprivation: I. relation to description of experience. *Percept. Mot. Skills*, 1964, **18**, 211–16.

RUFF, G. E., Levy, E. Z., and Thaler, V. H. Some influences on reaction to reduced sensory input. Unpublished manuscript, Stress and Fatigue Section, Aeromedical Lab., WADC, Dayton, Ohio, 1957.

RUFF, G. E., and Levy, E. Psychiatric research in space medicine. Paper read at American Psychiatric Association meeting, San Francisco, May, 1959.

RUFF, G. E., Levy, E. Z. and Thaler, V. H. Studies in isolation and confinement. *Aerospace Med.*, 1959, **30**, 599–604.

———. Factors influencing reactions to reduced sensory input. *In* P. Solomon *et al.* (Eds.), *Sensory deprivation.* Cambridge: Harvard University Press, 1961, 72–90.

SACKETT, G. P., Kieth-Lee, P., and Treat, R. Food versus perceptual complexity as rewards for rats previously subjected to sensory deprivation. *Science*, 1963, **141**, 518–20.

SALIMBENE. Cited in J. B. Ross and M. M. McLaughlin (Eds.), *A portable medieval reader.* New York: The Viking Press, 1946.

SANTUCCI, P. S., and Winokur, G. Brainwashing as a factor in psychiatric illness (a heuristic approach). *Arch. Neurol. and Psychiat.*, 1955, **74**, 15.

SARGANT, W. *Battle for the mind.* New York: Doubleday, 1957.

SATO, I., and Oyama, M. Studies on sensory deprivation I. III: Rorschach performance in sensory deprivation. *Tohoku Psychologia Folia*, 1963, **22**, 15–34.

SCHAEFER, T., Jr., and Bernick, N. The role of suggestion in "hallucinations" attributed to reduced sensory stimulation. Paper presented at Midwest Psychological Association meeting, Chicago, 1962.

SCHAFFER, H. R. Behavior under stress: neurophysiological hypothesis. *Psychol. Rev.*, 1954, **61**, 323–33.

SCHEIN, E. H. The Chinese indoctrination program for prisoners of war: a study of attempted "brainwashing." *Psychiat.*, 1956, **19**, 149–72.

———. Reaction patterns to severe, chronic stress in American Army prisoners of war of the Chinese. *J. Soc. Issues*, 1957, **13**, 21–30. (a)

———. Epilogue: something new in history? *J. Soc. Issues*, 1957, **13**, 56–60. (b)

———. Brainwashing and totalitarianism in modern society. *World Politics*, 1959, **11**, 430–41.

————. *Brainwashing.* Cambridge, Mass.: Center for International Studies, M.I.T., 1960. (a)

————. Interpersonal communication, group solidarity, and social influence. *Sociometry,* 1960, **23,** 148–61. (b)

————. *Coercive persuasion.* New York: W. W. Norton, 1961.

————. Man against man: brainwashing. *Corrective Psychiat. and J. Soc. Therapy,* 1962, **8,** 90–7.

SCHWARZ, L., and Huapaya, L. Distortions of human perception in semi-darkness: a phenomenological study. *Comprehensive Psychiat.,* 1964, **5,** 113–21.

SCOTT, J. M. *Portrait of an ice cap with human figures.* London: Chatto & Windus, 1953.

SCOTT, T. H. Intellectual effects of perceptual isolation. Unpublished doctoral dissertation, McGill University, 1954.

SCOTT, T. H., Bexton, W. H., Heron, W., and Doane, B. K. Cognitive effects of perceptual isolation. *Canad. J. Psychol.,* 1959, **13,** 200–9.

SEGAL, H. A. Initial psychiatric findings of recently repatriated prisoners of war. *Amer. J. Psychiat.,* 1954, **111,** 358–63.

SEGAL, J. Factors related to the collaboration and resistance behavior of U.S. Army POW's in Korea. *Hum. Resources Res. Off. Tech. Report* No. 33. Washington, D.C.: George Washington University Press, 1956.

SELLS, S. B., and Berry, C. H. *Human requirements for space travel.* Air University, 1961.

SENDEN, M. V. *Raum und Gestaltauffassung bei Operierten Blindgeborenen vor und Nach der Operation.* Leipzig: Barth, 1932.

SHURLEY, J. T. Profound experimental sensory isolation. *Amer. J. Psychiat.,* 1960, **117,.** 539–45.

————. Hallucinations in sensory deprivation and sleep deprivation. *In* L. J. West (Ed.), *Hallucinations.* New York: Grune & Stratton, 1962. (b)

————. Mental imagery in profound experimental sensory isolation. *In* L. J. West (Ed.), *Hallucinations.* New York: Grune & Stratton, 1962, 153–7. (a)

————. Problems and method in experimental sensory input alteration and invariance. *In* Tourlentes, T. T., Pollack, S. I., and Himwich, H. E. (Eds.), *Research approaches to psychiatric problems.* New York: Grune & Stratton, 1962, 145–60 (c.)

SILVERMAN, A. J., Cohen, S. I., Shmavonian, B. M., and Greenberg, G. Psychophysiological investigations in sensory deprivation: the body-field dimension. *Psychosom. Med.*, 1961, **23**, 48–62.

SILVERMAN, A. J., Cohen, S. I., Bressler, B., and Shmavonian, B. M. Hallucinations in sensory deprivation. *In* L. J. West (Ed.), *Hallucinations.* New York: Grune & Stratton, 1962, 124–34.

SINEVIRSKII, N. *Smersh.* Edited by Hill, K., and Hill, M. Translated by C. W. Boldyreff. New York: Henry Holt, 1950.

SIPPRELLE, C. N., Long, T. E., and Lucik, T. W. Qualitative changes in verbal response as a function of stimulus deprivation. *J. Clin. Psychol.*, 1963, **19**, 287–9.

SKINNER, B. F. *Science and human behavior.* New York: Macmillan, 1956.

SLOCUM, J. *Sailing around the world.* New York: Century, 1900.

SMALL, M. H. On some psychical relations of society and solitude. *Pedogical Sem.*, 1900, **7**, 13–69.

SMITH, S., and Lewty, W. Perceptual isolation using a silent room. *Lancet*, 1959, **2**, 342–5.

SOLOMON, P., Leiderman, P., Mendelson, J., and Wexler, D. Sensory deprivation: a review. *Amer. J. Psychiat.*, 1957, **114**, 357–63.

SOLOMON, P., Wexler, D., Mendelson, J., and Leiderman, P. Modification of the conscious state in sensory deprivation. Reprinted from special issue of *Excerpta Medica,* containing abstracts of papers read at joint meetings of the First International Congress of Neurological Sciences, Brussels, 1957 (July 21–28).

SOLOMON, P., Kubzansky, P., Leiderman, P., Mendelson, J., Trumbull, R., and Wexler, D. (Eds.), *Sensory deprivation: a symposium.* Cambridge: Harvard Univer. Press, 1961.

SOLOMON, P., and Mendelson, J. Hallucinations in sensory deprivation. *In* L. J. West (Ed.), *Hallucinations.* New York: Grune & Stratton, 1962.

SPITZ, R. A. "Hospitalism": an inquiry into the genesis of psychiatric conditions in early childhood. *Psychoanal. Stud. of Child.,* New York: International Universities Press, 1954, 53–74.

———. "Hospitalism": a follow-up report. *Psychoanal.*

Stud. of Child., New York: International Universities Press, 1955, 113.

STARE, F., Brown, J., and Orne, T. Demand characteristics in sensory deprivation studies. Unpublished seminar paper, Mass. Mental Health Center and Harvard University, 1959.

STEINKAMP, G. R., Hawkins, W. R., Hauty, G. T., Burwell, R. R., and Ward, J. E. Human experimentation in the space cabin simulator. *USAF School of Aviation Medicine,* 1959, No. 59–101.

STONE, L. J. A critique of studies of infant isolation. *Child Development,* 1954, **25**, 1–20.

STRASSMAN, H. D., Thaler, M. B., and Schein, E. H. A prisoner of war syndrome: apathy and reaction to severe stress. *Amer. J. Psychiat.,* 1956, **112**, 998–1003.

SUEDFELD, P. The effects of sensory deprivation and social isolation on performance of an unstructured cognitive task. Paper presented at Eastern Psychological Association meeting, New York, April, 1963.

———. Attitude manipulation in restricted environments: I. Conceptual structure and response to propaganda. *J. Abnorm. Soc. Psychol.,* 1964, **68**, 242–7.

———. Birth order of volunteers for sensory deprivation. *J. Abnorm. Soc. Psychol.,* 1964, **68**, 195–6.

SUEDFELD, P., Grissom, R. J., and Vernon, J. The effects of sensory deprivation and social isolation on the performance of an unstructured cognitive task. *Amer. J. Psychol.,* 1964, **77**, 111–15.

SURACI, A. Environmental stimulus reduction as a technique to effect the reactivation of crucial repressed memories. *J. Nerv. Ment. Dis.,* 1964, **138**, 172–80.

SVORAD, D. Certain manifestations of "sensory deprivation." *Cesk. Fysiol.,* 1960, **9**, 267.

SYKES, G. H. Men, merchants, and toughs: a study of reaction to imprisonment. *Soc. Probl.,* 1956, **4**, 130–8.

TENNIEN, M. *No secret is safe behind the bamboo curtain.* New York: Farrar, Straus and Young, 1952.

TEUBER, H. L. Sensory deprivation: facts in search of a theory: sensory deprivation, sensory suppression and agnosia: notes for a neurological theory. *J. Nerv. Ment. Dis.,* 1961, **132**, 32–40.

THOREAU, H. D. *Walden.* New York: W. W. Norton, 1951 edition.

THORIN, D. *The ride to Panmunjon.* Chicago: Regnery, 1956.

TROBRIDGE, G. *The life of Emanuel Swedenborg.* London: Swedenborg Press, 1945.

U.S. Congress, Senate. Committee on Government Operations, Permanent Subcommittee on Investigations. *Hearings, June 26, 1956.* Washington, D.C.: U.S. Govt. Print. Off., 1956.

———. Committee on Government Operations, Permanent Subcommittee on Investigations. *Communist interrogation, indoctrination and exploitation of American military and civilian prisoners.* 84th Congress, 2nd Session, Senate Report No. 2832, December 31, 1956. Washington, D.C.: U.S. Govt. Print. Off., 1957.

U.S. Department of the Army. *Communist interrogation, indoctrination and exploitation of prisoners of war.* Army pamphlet No. 30–101, May, 1956. Washington, D.C.: U.S. Govt. Print. Off., 1956.

U.S. Department of Defense. *POW: the fight continues after the battle.* The report of the Secretary of Defense's Advisory Committee on Prisoners of War, August, 1955. Washington, D.C.: U.S. Govt. Print. Off., 1955.

VERNON, J. A. Pain thresholds and time orientation in sensory deprivation. Unpublished manuscript, Psychol. Dept., Princeton University, 1959.

———. *Inside the black room.* New York: Clarkson N. Potter, 1964.

VERNON, J. A., and Hoffman, J. Effects of sensory deprivation on learning rate in human beings. *Science,* 1956, **123**, 1074.

VERNON, J. A., and McGill, T. E. The effect of sensory deprivation upon rote learning. *Amer. J. Psychol.,* 1957, **70**, 637–9.

VERNON, J. A., McGill, T. E., and Schiffman, H. Visual hallucinations during perceptual isolation. *Canad. J. Psychol.,* 1958, **12**, 30–4.

VERNON, J. A., McGill, T. E., Gulick, W. L., and Candland, D. K. Effect of sensory deprivation on some perceptual and motor skills. *Percept. Mot. Skills,* 1959, **9**, 91–7.

VERNON, J. A., and McGill, T. E. Utilization of visual stimulation during sensory deprivation. *Percept. Mot. Skills,* 1960, **11**, 214.

VERNON, J. A., McGill, T. E., Gulick, W. L. and Candland,

D. K. The effect of human isolation upon some perceptual and motor skills. *In* P. Solomon *et al.* (Eds.), *Sensory deprivation*. Cambridge, Mass.: Harvard University Press, 1961, 41–57.

VERNON, J. A., Marton, T., and Peterson, E. Sensory deprivation and hallucinations. *Science,* 1961, **133,** 1808–12.

VERNON, J. A., and McGill, T. E. Sensory deprivation and pain thresholds. *Science,* 1961, **133,** 330–1.

———. Sensory deprivation and hallucinations. *In* L. J. West (Ed.), *Hallucinations.* New York: Grune & Stratton, 1962.

———. Time estimations during sensory deprivation. *J. Gen. Psychol.,* 1963, **69,** 11–18.

VOSBURG, R. L. Sensory deprivation and isolation. *Bull. West. Psychiat. Inst.,* 1958 (Oct.).

VOSBURG, R. L., Fraser, N., and Guehl, J., Jr. Imagery sequence in sensory deprivation. *AMA Arch. Gen. Psychiat.,* 1960, **2,** 356–357.

WALTERS, C., Shurley, J., and Parsons, O. Difference in male and female response to underwater sensory deprivation. *J. Nerv. Ment. Dis.,* 1962, **135,** 302–10.

———. Male-female differences in underwater sensory isolation. *Brit. J. Psychiat.,* 1964, **110,** 290–308.

WALTERS, R. H., and Quinn, M. J. The effects of social and sensory deprivation on autokinetic judgments. *J. Pers.,* 1960, **28,** 210–19.

WENDT, R. H., Lindsley, D. F., and Adey, W. R. Self-maintained visual stimulation in monkeys after long-term visual deprivation. *Science,* 1963, **139,** 336–8.

WEST, L. J. United States Air Force prisoners of the Chinese Communists. *In* Group for the Advancement of Psychiatry, *Methods of forceful indoctrination: observations and interviews. GAP Symposium* No. 4. New York: GAP Publications Office, July, 1957, 270–84.

———. Psychiatric aspects of training for honorable survival as a prisoner of war. *Amer. J. Psychiat.,* 1958, **115,** 329–36.

WEST, L. J. (Ed.). *Hallucinations.* New York: Grune & Stratton, 1962, iii and 295.

WEXLER, D., Mendelson, J., Leiderman, P. H., and Solomon, P. Sensory deprivation: a technique for studying the psychiatric aspects of stress. *AMA Arch. Neurol. Psychiat.,* 1958, **79,** 225–33.

WEYBREW, B. B., and Parker, J. W. Bibliography of sensory deprivation, isolation and confinement. *USA Med. Res. Lab. Memo. Rep.* No. 60–1, 1960.

WHEATON, J. L. Fact and fancy in sensory deprivation studies. *Aeromed. Rev.*, 1959, 5. School of Aviation Medicine, U.S.A.F., Brooks AFB, Texas.

WINOKUR, G. The germ warfare statements: a synthesis of a method for the extortion of false confessions. *J. Nerv. Ment. Dis.*, 1955, 122, 65–72.

WOLFF, H. G. Commitment and resistance. Washington, D.C.: *Bureau of Soc. Sci. Res., Inc.*, January, 1959. *Study SR* 177-D, *Special Report* No. 3.

ZIMMER, H., and Meltzer, M. L. *An annotated bibliography of literature relevant to the interrogation process.* Washington, D.C.: Georgetown Univer. Med. Center, 1957.

ZINGG, R. M. Feral man and extreme cases of social isolation. *Amer. J. Psychol.*, 1940, 53, 487–517.

———. More about the "Baboon Boy" of South Africa. *Amer. J. Psychol.*, 1940, 53, 455–61.

———. India's wolf children. *Sci. Amer.*, 1941, March, 135–7.

ZISKIND, E. Isolation stress in medical and mental illness. *J. Amer. Med. Assn.*, 1958, 168, 1427–31.

———. A second look at sensory deprivation. *J. Nerv. Ment. Dis.*, 1964, 138, 223–32.

———. Significance of symptoms in sensory deprivation experiments due to methodological procedure. *In* Wortis, J. (Ed.), *Recent advances in biological psychiatry*, Vol. 6. New York: Grune & Stratton, 1964 (in press).

ZISKIND, E., Jones, H., Filante, W., and Goldberg, J. Observations on mental symptoms in eye patched patients: hypnogogic symptoms in sensory deprivation. *Amer. J. Psychiat.*, 1960, 116, 893–900.

ZISKIND, E., and Augsburg, T. Hallucinations in sensory deprivation: method or madness? *Science*, 1962, 137, 992–3.

ZISKIND, E., Graham, R., Kuniobu, L., and Ainsworth, R. The hypnoid syndrome in sensory deprivation. In Wortis, J. (Ed.), *Recent advances in biological psychiatry*, Vol. 5. New York: Grune & Stratton, 1963, 331–46.

ZUBEK, J. P. Counteracting effects of physical exercises performed during prolonged perceptual deprivation. *Science*, 1963, 142, 504–6. (a)

———. Pain sensitivity as a measure of perceptual deprivation tolerance. *Percept. Mot. Skills,* 1963, 17, 641–2. (b)

ZUBEK, J. P., Sansom, W., and Prysiaznuik, A. Intellectual changes during prolonged perceptual isolation. (darkness and silence). *Canad. J. Psychol.,* 1960, 14, 233–43.

ZUBEK, J. P., Pyshkar, D., Sansom, W., and Gowing, J. Perceptual changes after prolonged perceptual isolation. *Canad. J. Psychol.,* 1961, 83–100.

ZUBEK, J. P., Aftanas, M., Hasek, J., Sansom, W., Schluderman, E., Wilgosh, I., and Winocur, G. Intellectual and perceptual changes during prolonged perceptual deprivation. *Percept. Mot. Skills,* 1962, 15, 171–98 (Monogr. Suppl. 1-V15).

ZUBEK, J. P., Aftanas, M., Kovach, K., Wilgosh, L., and Winocur, G. Effects of severe immobilization of the body on intellectual and perceptual processes. *Canad. J. Psychol.,* 1963, 17, 118–33.

ZUBER, J. P., and Welch, G. Electroencephalographic changes after prolonged sensory and perceptual deprivation. *Science,* 1963, 139, 1209–10.

ZUBEK, J. P., and Wilgosh, L. Prolonged immobilization of the body: changes in performance and in the electroencephalogram. *Science,* 1963, 140, 306–8.

ZUCKERMAN, M. Perceptual isolation as a stress situation. *Arch. Gen. Psychiat.,* 1964, 26, 255–76.

ZUCKERMAN, M., Albright, R. J., Marks, C. S., and Miller, G. L. Stress and hallucinatory effects of perceptual isolation and confinement. *Psychol. Monogr.,* 1962, 76, (Whole No. 549).

ZUCKERMAN, M., and Cohen, N. Is suggestion the source of reported visual sensations in perceptual isolation? *J. Abnorm. Soc. Psychol.,* 1964, 68, 655–60.

———. Sources of reports of visual and auditory sensations in perceptual isolation experiments. *Psychol. Bull.,* 1964, 62, 1–20.

ZUCKERMAN, M., Levine, S., and Biase, D. V. Stress responses in total and partial perceptual isolation. *Psychosom. Med.,* 1964, 26, 250–60.

Index «